OUR NEW MEXICO

Our New Mexico

A TWENTIETH CENTURY HISTORY

NARRATIVE TEXT BY
Calvin A. Roberts, Ph.D.

EDITORIAL ADVISOR
David Holtby, Ph.D.

COMPILED BY
Lincoln Bramwell, Ph.D. candidate in History,
Sonia Dickey, Ph.D. candidate in History, and
Lisa Pacheco, Ph.D. candidate in Anthropology
CENTER FOR REGIONAL STUDIES INTERNS AND
EDITORIAL ASSISTANTS AT THE
UNIVERSITY OF NEW MEXICO PRESS

EDUCATIONAL CONSULTANT ON THE BOOK
Midge Y. Arthur, M.A.

EDUCATIONAL CONSULTANT ON THE TEACHER/STUDENT MATERIALS

UNIVERSITY OF NEW MEXICO PRESS ❧ ALBUQUERQUE

PRINTED IN THE UNITED STATES OF AMERICA

13   12   11   10   09   4   5   6   7   8   9

ISBN-13: 978-0-8263-4008-5
ISBN-10: 0-8263-4008-3

Book and cover design and type composition
    by Kathleen Sparkes

Cover photograph: The New Mexico Wind
    Energy Center, photo by Norman Johnson,
    courtesy of PNM

This book is typeset in Janson. The body type is
    10.5/16 and the excerpt text is 11.5/16

The display type is Univers family and Janson family.

CONTENTS

Introduction

"Why another semester of New Mexico history?" you ask. Maybe you wonder, "Has anything happened that is new since the other two times I took it?"

To answer the first question, let me ask you one: "How many times have you taken courses in math, English, or science?" More times than you have studied New Mexico's history, right? If you have gone to school in New Mexico since fourth grade, you have twice before studied the state's history.

Do you remember what you studied in math, English, or science in fourth grade and seventh grade? It was at a different level and you learned basics, right? Now you are in ninth grade. You are still taking some or all of those subjects again. Why? The answer is the same as the answer to why you are taking another class in New Mexico history. You are now going to build on and expand what you learned in your earlier classes. You are moving into a more advanced level and well beyond the basics.

You also asked if anything new has happened since you last studied New Mexico history. Again, to answer the question I need to ask you one: "Are you the same person in every way as when you were in seventh or fourth grade?" Of course you are not. You understand and know much more now than you did a couple of years ago. You are maturing.

You are also using new skills. One of these skills is critical thinking. In fact, this course is all about developing critical thinking. So what does it mean to use "critical thinking" in studying New Mexico history? Two traits of critical thinking will be most frequently used. The first is grasping what is most important to know in a selection. The second is understanding point of view, or interpretation.

Your textbook, *Our New Mexico: A Twentieth Century History*, is organized to challenge you to think independently. It does so by having you read at two different levels. One level is for information; the other is for intent or point of view. For these latter readings, you are going to be asking and answering questions and using lots of critical thinking skills.

The first level of reading is found in brief narratives. These give you information to introduce topics or help you put events and people's responses into context. They were written by a high school teacher who spent thirty years teaching New Mexico's students.

Then there are fifty-six in-depth discussions about topics in New Mexico's history. In these you are going to explore new ideas, evaluate what is being presented, analyze it for a point of view or interpretation, and see connections and similarities as well as contrasts among the discussions. These fifty-six accounts are written by people who have spent years studying the topic about which they write.

This book is about New Mexico's history since statehood in 1912. It has eleven chapters organized into sections in which you have a brief overview of a period or a topic. These are followed by a selection in which an expert tells you more about the subject based on their years of study. *Our New Mexico* has two goals: 1) to help you learn more about New Mexico's history over the past one hundred years; and 2) to have you apply critical thinking skills.

Your teacher is going to help you with both the learning and the critical thinking. So will your classmates. Together you will have activities, worksheets, and other class exercises to help you succeed. At the end of the semester, you will be able to read and discuss ideas and points of view that are important to understand because you live in New Mexico. You are going to study the twentieth century to help prepare you for a productive life in the twenty-first century.

The future in New Mexico is shaped by what has gone before. In a few years you will be out of high school and beginning to make a life for yourself. Your future is linked to and a part of what is ahead for New Mexico. You will be impacted by and have to deal with issues all New Mexicans face. This book introduces you to three themes important in New Mexico's past, present, and future. These are resources, culture, and continuity amid change.

These three themes may seem remote to your interests today, but when you finish this semester you will understand why they are ever-present and important. These three themes are at the foundation of everything else in New Mexicans' daily lives. Resources, culture, and continuity amid change define who we are and what we can become. Let's look at each of the three briefly.

Resources include water and land and the wise use of each. Think about this: Can you survive without water? Can you travel around without having your trip conform to where roads are placed, homes, restaurants, and schools are built, or where fences or natural barriers like rivers, canyons, or mountains exist? How New Mexicans built on the land created patterns for how people move about today. The water found in the state's rivers, lakes, reservoirs, and irrigation canals is part of the natural landscape or environment. The lands over and through which water flows are the other key part—farm and ranch lands, towns and cities, valleys, mountains, or deserts. These, too, are essential elements in the natural landscape or environment. Understanding how people have used the state's landscape will help you make choices in your life about the future of those resources.

Culture is all around us and it is very diverse. It is all the people from many backgrounds who live in New Mexico. It is also the way these people express themselves. It is found in their language, their creativity in art and writing, their celebrations, their work and accomplishments, and all the ways that blend each person into a group. New Mexico is a multicultural state, perhaps one of the most diverse in all of the United States. Our cultural heritage enriches us. By studying it, you will better see how your life is part of traditions or patterns of living inherited from earlier generations.

The third and final theme is continuity amid change. This simply means that while things change around us, underneath these changes is a level where things are long-lasting and fundamentally unaltered. Anything that is long-enduring is continuity in our life. Think of it this way: you started going to school years ago. You have had many teachers, sat in many difficult classrooms, known many other kids, and had some good times and maybe a few you would rather forget. All these are aspects of change in your life. But the continuity is that you are still learning and you are still growing up. Continuities, then, tend to be processes or stages. Change tends to be the specifics or the details that swirl around the processes.

Now we are going to combine the ideas introduced so far. We are going to do so through two sample selections. Each is an example of what you will read throughout *Our New Mexico*. Each selection also discusses one or more of the themes of resources, culture, and continuity amid change. These selections also require you to think critically about what is being said. You need to read these with two questions in mind: "What is it I need to know or remember?" and "What is their point of view, and how would I put it into my own words?"

The first reading talks about tourism in New Mexico by looking at our capital city, Santa Fe. Tourism is a major industry in the state and very important to our economy. But tourism brings in more than money. Tourism can change people, and this reading talks about tourism's impact on culture and makes us aware of continuity amid change.

In 1999 the 287th Santa Fe Fiesta occurred. Here is what one person saw and thought about as he watched the parade.

SELECTION FROM

Santa Fe Hispanic Culture
Preserving Identity in a Tourist Town

The afternoon of Sunday, September 12, 1999, was a typically sunny day in Santa Fe, New Mexico. As I sat on the curb in front of the Santa Fe Public Library on Washington Avenue, I could not help but smile at the scene that passed before my eyes. I was witnessing the *Desfile de la Fiesta*, more commonly known as the Historical/Hysterical Parade, one of the highlights of the 287th Fiesta de Santa Fe.

To the uninitiated, the scene might have seemed surreal. The parade procession included the 1999 Fiesta Queen (who was my sister); the honorary Don Diego De Vargas and his *Cuadrilla* (staff); local politicians waving to the crowds in souped-up, lowrider cars; an Elvis impersonator; a four-piece band in the back of a pickup truck playing "La Bamba"; bodybuilders lifting weights on a flatbed truck; high school marching bands; floats advertising local businesses including a funeral home, pizza place, and motorcycle shop; a huge snorting papier-maché bull with flashing eyes promoting the Rodeo de Santa Fe; senior citizens in buses throwing candy to the crowd; and lots of horses.

This colorful collage that paraded through the streets of downtown Santa Fe during the 1999 Fiesta was in some ways a reflection of the nature and character of the Santa Fe that has evolved through the years and that exists today.

Santa Fe is a city of ancient traditions, but also of "invented traditions." It is deeply influenced by its cultural roots. At the same time, it has been willing to reshape its cultural symbols for sale to the highest bidder. It is both a small town and rather cosmopolitan. In short, Santa Fe is a tourist town. It is a community that loves its roots and simultaneously generates its livelihood from those roots.

As a native Hispanic resident of Santa Fe, I have witnessed these contradictions and experienced this unique blend of fact and fantasy. (Pp. xi–xii)

—*Andrew Leo Lovato*

In terms of the two questions you always need to keep in mind, let's see what we can offer as answers. First we want to figure out what is it this writer wants us to remember after reading this selection? One answer would be that he really likes the Santa Fe Fiesta but that the city uses the Fiesta in some ways that make him uncomfortable. You may have come up with a different answer to the question. That is fine as long as it is the result of you thinking about and basing your answer on what he said.

The second question we need to answer is this: What is his point of view, what is the meaning to him of what he sees? Sometimes it is easiest to begin answering this question by finding a phrase or sentence that you believe sums up his interpretation. Let's look at this sentence: "It is a community that loves its roots and simultaneously generates its livelihood from those roots."

How would you put that in your own words? One way is to see how it relates to one or more of the three major themes: resources, culture, and continuity amid change. This excerpt certainly relates to the latter two. So, we can say that Santa Fe uses its cultural heritage to honor its past; however, it does so in ways that appeal to many diverse people. It sells them an event that is "a unique blend of fact and fantasy."

What is important in critical thinking is asking and answering questions. Let me ask you five more questions about this selection. What most struck you about it? Were you surprised that while the author took pride in seeing his sister as Fiesta Queen, he also thought about what the Fiesta revealed about his city? What is meant by the statement that Santa Fe is a city of "fact and fantasy"? What examples does he give to support that claim? How are politicians in lowrider cars and bodybuilders lifting weights on a flatbed truck "a reflection of the nature and culture of Santa Fe that has evolved through the years and that exists today"? An exercise in the student activity materials provided by your teacher will help you think about each question. The process of discussing different possible answers with classmates is an important part, too, in critical thinking.

The second selection in the next few paragraphs is quite different in tone from the first. Throughout *Our New Mexico* you will find that the authors take different approaches to their topics. Some are personal accounts; others are summaries of historical events; and still others are new ways of looking at familiar things. This selection is the latter. It gives you a way to think about how different people in New Mexico attach value and importance to land. It also relates these cultural views to understanding the Zia symbol in our state flag. Finally, it touches on all three of the themes: resources, culture, and continuity amid change.

SELECTION FROM
The Lore of New Mexico

New Mexican lore about land or place focuses on centers and peripheries, or edges. The Indian world is bounded by mountains and centered in ceremonials stemming from the place of emergence. Hispanos erected crosses and constructed plazas surrounded by common lands for grazing and wood gathering. Anglo ranchers and homesteaders fenced domains centered on springs, windmills, and later crossroads of commerce. Such settlements became sanctuaries, protecting and sustaining their inhabitants. Beyond their bounds were the wilds, the elemental, and the alien.

Herders, hunters, trappers, miners, and prospectors regularly ventured onto the peripheries and, upon their return from "the wilds" or "below" were often viewed as special, marked by their outside experiences. Those who, like raiders, warriors, traders, and freighters, periodically crossed and recrossed boundaries between centers of people were also marked as heroic figures. Whether traveling trackless wastes, corn pollen ways, foot trails, horse and cart roads, highways, or rails, these heroes engaged in profound commerce— a communication of powerfully expressive and materially important symbols, goods, plants, and animals. Their commerce is a voluntary journeying, far different from the dislocation of captives and the conquered and encroached upon. Nevertheless, those who brave the wilds, those who communicate across boundaries, and those who are uprooted bring into focus traditional notions of settlement and centering.

These traditional notions have also been embodied in the Zia symbol on the New Mexico flag. Seen from Indian, Hispanic, and Anglo perspectives, it incorporates fundamental concepts of settlement and movement. Indians' sacred space is centered inward along corn pollen roads and surrounded by mountains, rivers, oceans, and under and upper worlds. For Hispanos, the lines form a cross, symbolic of the central Christian sacrifice, which makes sacred and establishes place and people wherever it is properly raised. Anglos view the sixteen lines as radiating outward—whether along roads and rails to homes and commercial centers elsewhere, down into mines and pits, or out into space. (Pp. 229–30)

—Marta Weigle and Peter White

A thought-provoking few paragraphs, right? I bet you will look at the Zia symbol differently after reading the selection. In fact, that is maybe the piece's main point. To help you see familiar things in new ways and understand that the meaning we attach to things springs from our traditions and values. This is probably the most challenging selection in *Our New Mexico*. I wanted to introduce it early on so you can think about it during the semester. As you gain confidence in your critical thinking skills, come back to this piece. Keep asking yourself what it is the writers want you to know and what is their point of view or interpretation. Your answers may be different from the first time you read it, which is a sign of your growth and skill in critical thinking. A change in answers also means you are seeing and understanding New Mexico and its history at a deeper level. That is the purpose of *Our New Mexico*.

So, why are you once again studying New Mexico history? The understanding and insights you gain in this class will enrich your life and prepare you for the challenges of citizenship.

David Holtby, Ph.D.
Visiting Scholar
Center for Regional Studies
University of New Mexico

NEW MEXICO EVENTS

New Mexico is a state	1912
Villa raids Columbus	1916
Bursum Bill is defeated	1924
Great Depression begins	1929
New Deal relief begins	1933
Atomic bomb is tested	1945
Alianza is active	1966
Blue Lake returned to Taos Indians	1970
Sunbelt growth seen	1974
Population tops 1.8 million	2000

WORLD EVENTS

Panama Canal opens	1914
U.S. enters World War I	1917
Lindbergh flies the Atlantic	1927
U.S. enters World War II	1941
Cold War begins	1945
Sputnik launched	1957
Men walk on the moon	1969
First personal computer built	1975
Berlin Wall falls	1989
War on terrorism begins	2001

PART ONE

New Mexico Becomes a State

Introduction

On October 11, 1911, Charles Walsh looked down on the Rio Grande. The river flowed just a few hundred feet below. Seated on the lower wing of his flimsy Curtiss biplane, Walsh flew south down the valley. Then he swung around at the Barelas Bridge and flew back north, landing at the territorial fairgrounds near Old Town in Albuquerque. His entire flight took ten minutes to cover twelve miles. In those few minutes, though, Walsh made history. He completed the first airplane flight ever in New Mexico.

Over the next few days New Mexicans flocked to the fairgrounds. Spectators in the grandstands gaped as Walsh dropped fake bombs on the outline of a battleship below. Shopkeepers and shoppers rushed into the streets whenever the biplane flew over the city. On his last flight, the pilot took along a passenger. In circling the fairgrounds that day, the pilot, it is said, set a world record. It was the first time ever a passenger had been lifted and carried on a plane at an altitude of over 5,000 feet above sea level.

Indeed, New Mexico was entering a time of change and challenge. In this chapter you will learn how New Mexico became a state and became more involved in world affairs. You will also learn how New Mexico welcomed the arrival of artists and revived local arts and crafts. At the same time, Pueblo peoples united once again to protect their land while New Mexicans, like all Americans, suffered from the hard times of the 1930s.

CHAPTER ONE

An Invitation to Statehood

Congress Invites New Mexico to Become a State

By 1900 most New Mexicans wanted statehood. They had waited for it since 1848. During this time several factors had hurt their chances. The very name "New Mexico" had raised eyebrows. Was this some "foreign land" trying to slip into the Union? Some opponents to statehood for New Mexico pointed to a lack of public schools. Others claimed that New Mexico's Hispanic citizens were not "Americans." They did not trust the loyalty of citizens who spoke Spanish. Lawless events, such as the Lincoln County War, also painted a poor picture of New Mexico. For these and other reasons statehood was delayed.

Finally, in 1910 Congress acted. It passed an enabling act telling New Mexicans to draw up a constitution. They could do so knowing that Congress was ready to grant statehood. The constitution would outline state government. Then, it would go to the voters for approval. It would also have to be approved by Congress and the president. Only then could New Mexico become a state. The voters and Congress approved, and on January 6, 1912, President William Howard Taft made it official. He declared New Mexico to be the forty-seventh state. The many years of waiting for statehood had ended.

SELECTION FROM
The Far Southwest, 1846–1912
A Territorial History

The final struggle to gain statehood for . . . New Mexico lasted from 1901 to 1912 and was the longest sustained admission fight in American territorial history. It also took place under conditions that no other territory had ever experienced. The movement became entangled in three great national debates. The first of these concerned the continuing argument growing out of the Spanish-American War. Should America be an imperial nation with colonies or should it accept the new possessions of Puerto Rico and the Philippines as an eventual part of the American Union?

The second debate concerned the use and disposition of national resources in the Far Southwest. Between 1901 and 1912 millions of acres were withdrawn from the public domain. The eventual result was that . . . 12 percent of those acres in New Mexico were set aside as national forests. Since nearly every prominent rancher in New Mexico was hit by these measures, the resentment and political agitation that resulted kept the territory in a turmoil for ten years. . . .

Finally, the Republican Party and the entire country were caught up in a reform movement known as Progressivism. Some supported it and others did not. In Congress the growing split between Republicans over Progressivism greatly hindered the statehood cause. To gain admission, therefore, the statehood politicians had to thread their way past the heritage of the Spanish-American War, the conservation crusade, and the Progressive movement, before they could claim victory. . . .

The Arizona and New Mexico admission fights demonstrated the familiar struggle of a region acting to resist outside authority, which was attempting to standardize and force conformity. In this case the authority wanted adherence to national Republican and Progressive ideals. . . .

The struggle for statehood also illustrates another classic pattern in American political history: how national issues and fads can so vitally affect local causes. Not only did admission become entangled in the prohibition issue and involved in the debates over women's rights and new ideas like the initiative and the referendum, but it was clouded by the free-silver controversy, war, conservation, land policies, feelings about the new immigration, and anti-southwestern attitudes. The regional struggle between East and West and the political struggle between conservative and reform-minded Republicans in the 1910 Congress played vital roles as well. All in all, then, the admission debate mirrored American prejudices and preoccupations at the turn of the century. It also demonstrated how the concerns of the "metropolis" and the nation could affect the fortunes of the "province. . . . "

President Taft admitted New Mexico to the Union on January 6, 1912. A long and colorful but often painful era of political apprenticeship had come to an end for the Spanish borderlands of the American Southwest. American habits, customs, and democratic institutions—such as the two-party system, public schools, elective office, county government, and secular courts—were now established there. While Congress never had a real territorial policy, it had always set these conditions as a minimal requirement. . . . The fact of statehood symbolized that a satisfactory "Americanization" had been achieved. But in the process the unique qualities of the Far Southwest and the long persistence of the frontier period there had greatly affected and enriched the unfolding chronicle of American history. (Pp. 423–36)

—Howard R. Lamar

The Constitution Outlines State Government

Most of the constitution of 1910 remains in effect today. It has been changed over the years, but the basic outline of state government it laid out is still used today. Under this constitution New Mexico has three branches of government. These three are the executive, the legislative, and the judicial. Each one has special powers. The executive branch carries out the laws. The legislative branch makes the laws. The judicial branch says what the laws mean.

The governor heads the executive branch. State governors have many jobs to perform. They can approve laws passed by the legislature. They also have the power to veto laws. The power to veto means the governor can say "no" to an act passed by the legislature. Then the act will not become a law. The governor also appoints heads of the many departments of state government. Daily the governor serves as spokesman for the state. Today governors and other executive officials are elected for terms of four years.

SELECTION FROM

Civics for New Mexicans

Like Presidents of the United States, governors of New Mexico serve four-year terms. Also like Presidents, New Mexico's governors wear many hats. In general, governors wear five hats. These are executive, legislative, judicial, and ceremonial hats, and the hat of their political party.

As the chief executive officer of New Mexico, governors have the job of carrying out the laws. Their power is not nearly as great as that of Presidents of the United States. They do not appoint or choose the people who share executive power with them. Some very important decision-makers are elected. For example, the attorney general, the secretary of state, the auditor, and the treasurer are elected by the voters of the state. Governors, however, have power to appoint some state officers. Many state officials owe their jobs to governors.

To a great extent, state laws are enforced by city police and county sheriffs. Governors do control two groups that help them enforce state laws and maintain order. The New Mexico Constitution gives them emergency power to call upon the New Mexico National Guard. Governors are the commander-in-chief of the New Mexico National Guard. They can also call upon the state police to help in some emergencies. (P. 45)

—Susan A. Roberts, Betty L. Waugh, and Anne H. Gonzales

SELECTION FROM

New Mexico Blue Book, 2003–2004

CHRONOLOGICAL LIST OF STATE GOVERNORS

1912–1916	William C. McDonald	(D)
1917	Ezequial C. de Baca	(D)
1917–1918	Washington E. Lindsey	(R)
1919–1920	Octaviano A. Larrazolo	(R)
1921–1922	Merritt C. Mechem	(R)
1923–1924	James F. Hinkle	(D)
1925–1926	Arthur T. Hannett	(D)

1927–1928	Richard C. Dillon	(R)
1929–1930	Richard C. Dillon	(R)
1931–1932	Arthur Seligman	(D)
1933	Arthur Seligman	(D)
1933–1934	Andrew D. Hockenhull	(D)
1935–1936	Clyde Tingley	(D)
1937–1938	Clyde Tingley	(D)
1939–1940	John E. Miles	(D)
1941–1942	John E. Miles	(D)
1943–1944	John J. Dempsey	(D)
1945–1946	John J. Dempsey	(D)
1947–1948	Thomas J. Mabry	(D)
1949–1950	Thomas J. Mabry	(D)
1951–1952	Edwin L. Mechem	(R)
1953–1954	Edwin L. Mechem	(R)
1955–1956	John F. Simms, Jr.	(D)
1957–1958	Edwin L. Mechem	(R)
1959–1960	John Burroughs	(D)
1961–1962	Edwin L. Mechem	(R)
1962	Tom Bolack	(R)
1963–1964	Jack M. Campbell	(D)
1965–1966	Jack M. Campbell	(D)
1967–1968	David F. Cargo	(R)
1969–1970	David F. Cargo	(R)

(Law changed to allow 4-year terms.)

1971–1974	Bruce King	(D)
1975–1978	Jerry Apodaca	(D)
1979–1982	Bruce King	(D)
1983–1986	Toney Anaya	(D)
1987–1990	Garrey Carruthers	(R)

(Law changed to allow consecutive terms.)

1991–1994	Bruce King	(D)
1995–1998	Gary E. Johnson	(R)
1999–2002	Gary E. Johnson	(R)
2003–2006*	Bill Richardson	(D)

*Projected end-of-term date (Pp. 122–23)

—*Rebecca Vigil-Giron, Secretary of State*

SELECTION FROM

New Mexico Blue Book, 2003–2004

Governor Bill Richardson was elected Governor of New Mexico in 2002 by the largest margin of any candidate since 1964.... Governor Richardson also served as our Congressman for fifteen years for northern New Mexico, representing the 3rd Congressional District, beginning in 1983. Governor Richardson then served, in 1997, as the U.S. ambassador to the United Nations. Following, he was U.S. Secretary of Energy from 1998–2000. Governor Richardson has also been nominated four times for the Nobel Peace Prize. (P. v)

—Rebecca Vigil-Giron, Secretary of State

The legislature has two parts. These are the senate and the house of representatives. Voters elect senators and representatives from districts around the state. Together they introduce and pass laws. A two-thirds majority of both the senate and the house is required to overturn a governor's veto of a law. Senators serve four-year terms. Representatives serve two-year terms. Today, there are forty-two state senators and seventy representatives.

SELECTION FROM

Civics for New Mexicans

New Mexico is divided into forty-two senate voting districts. Each of these districts has about the same number of people. The people in each senate district elect *one* member to the New Mexico State Senate.

New Mexico is also divided into seventy house districts. Each of these districts has about the same number of people. Each district elects *one* member to the New Mexico House of Representatives.

In this way, equal numbers of people—ranchers as well as city dwellers—get equal representation in the New Mexico State Legislature. A large county like Bernalillo has many districts. Several counties with small populations combine to form just one district.

New Mexico House members must be twenty-one years of age. Senators must be at least twenty-five. A legislator must be a citizen of the United States, and he or she must live in the district represented.

Members of the New Mexico Legislature are not paid a salary. The New Mexico Constitution says that each member is to be paid for his or her expenses during each session. In addition, each member is paid for travel to Santa Fe and back home again once each session.

According to law, the legislature meets in Santa Fe on the third Tuesday in January of each year. In odd-numbered years, the session is for sixty days. In even-numbered years, the session is for thirty days.

The major job of the New Mexico State Legislature is to pass laws. Each legislator is expected to care about what is good for the whole state. But each legislator is also concerned about the wishes of the voters in his or her own district. Legislators are concerned also about the people who helped them to get elected. These people sometimes want favors from legislators in return for their help at election time. They may be farmers, labor leaders, oil producers, or educators. They try to help the legislators decide to vote for or against certain bills.

Most of the work of the New Mexico Legislature, like the work of the United States Congress, is done in committees. Early in each session, the committee assignments are made. Legislators are assigned to the committees that they prefer, if possible. A legislator may serve on only two of the standing committees.

In committees, the legislators study bills. They hold public hearings in order to find out how different people or groups feel about the bills. During the sixty-day session, the legislature must consider as many as a thousand bills. It is nearly impossible for each legislator to be an "expert" on that many bills. Therefore, the committees serve an important function by giving each bill a fair hearing. (Pp. 40–42)

—Susan A. Roberts, Betty L. Waugh, and Anne H. Gonzales

The state courts make up the judicial branch. This branch of government decides cases. District courts are the main trial courts. They hear most cases the first time. A supreme court and a court of appeals review the decisions of the district courts. New Mexico judges today are either appointed by the governor or elected to office by the voters.

Hispanics and Women Are Active in State Politics

Almost all main offices in state government are elected. From the start Hispanics ran for state offices. Voters elected Ezequiel C. de Baca as the state's first lieutenant governor. In 1916 they chose him to be the second governor. Two years later, a second Hispanic, Octaviano Larrazolo, won election as governor. Ten years later New Mexicans elected him the first Hispanic in the United States Senate. Hispanic candidates also had other successes, winning three of the first six elections for United States Representative.

In 1920 Hispanic and Anglo women in New Mexico gained the right to vote. They, too, quickly entered politics. In 1922 Soledad Chacón won election as New Mexico's secretary of state. Women have held that office ever since. For a time in 1924, Chacón was the first female acting governor of New Mexico. At that time both the governor and lieutenant governor were out of the state.

Another woman, Nina Otero-Warren, also made her mark in politics. Her family had long been involved in government. Her first cousin Miguel A. Otero had been a territorial governor. In 1917 Otero-Warren became a leading spokesperson for giving the right to vote to women. Because of her efforts and the efforts of others, women did get the vote in 1920.

In 1922 she ran for the United States House of Representatives. She lost this election, but she stayed active in government. In the 1920s she served as school superintendent in Santa Fe. In that job she worked hard to improve New Mexico schools. She once wrote, "I believe the greatest need in our country is education." Because of the efforts of Otero-Warren and Chacón, women have continued to play an important role in New Mexico politics and government. Nina Otero-Warren and other Hispanics active in education and politics also worked on behalf of bilingual education and preserving the Spanish language as a valued part of New Mexico's heritage.

SELECTION FROM

The Language of Blood
The Making of Spanish-American Identity in New Mexico, 1880s–1930s

Self-described "Spanish American" professionals sought fervently to instill an ethnic pride among *Nuevomexicanos* of all classes by way of education. This effort was most evident among educators who, from the 1890s through the

1930s, fought to preserve Spanish-language instruction and to impart among schoolchildren a pride in their native language and Spanish heritage.

For much of the nineteenth century, the philosophy underpinning public education dated to early reformers such as Horace Mann. Mann viewed "common schools" as a means of eliminating social problems, particularly poverty and class divisions. By equipping students with "good work habits" and a common faith in the political system and the vote, public schools would "disarm the poor of their hostility towards the rich" and would "prevent" poverty. In the early years of the twentieth century, however, public education was conceived as a vehicle for molding students into "worker-citizens" and for integrating them into the new industrial order.

With the passage of a major school law in 1891, public education in New Mexico became more accessible to families of modest or moderate means. Leaders of the territory, including Governor Lebaron Bradford Prince, viewed this achievement as one step toward preparing New Mexico for statehood. Prince called for the creation of more public schools and the establishment of a normal school for teachers, who were to receive uniform—though minimal—preparation, examination, and certification. Importantly, the 1891 law allowed for grade-school teachers to instruct students in either English or Spanish. Most schools and teachers taught in English, yet about one-third taught in Spanish. This provision gave official sanction to the use of Spanish in public schools alongside and, sometimes, in place of English. But it was also the source of controversy for years to come.

One of the most vocal advocates of this idea was New Mexico's Superintendent of Public Instruction Amado Cháves. In his 1894 report to the governor, Superintendent Cháves declared that there simply were not enough teachers who knew Spanish to adequately teach Spanish-speaking students, and that, as a result, these students were lagging behind their English-speaking classmates. He called for more bilingual teachers and, in 1896, urged that New Mexico's higher institutions require their graduates to complete a course in Spanish. He went on to say that "[i]t is a crime . . . to rob the children of New Mexico of . . . [their] language which is theirs by birth-right. English and Spanish are to go hand in hand in our schools, and only the height of bigotry and supine ignorance can ever affirm that the possessor of more than one language is unfit to be a good citizen." Cháves's successors, Plácido Sandoval, Manuel C. de Baca, and José Francisco Cháves, echoed this conviction. Like Amado Cháves, they believed that English was an indispensable component of U.S. citizenship, but that citizenship was not tied to the exclusive use of the English language. A true democratic republic, they suggested in their reports to the governor, allowed for the expression of one's native language in addition to English.

Beginning in 1905, *Nuevomexicano* superintendents were being replaced by Anglo-American ones who were less receptive to bilingualism, if not wholly opposed to it. At this time, Congress was still deliberating statehood for New Mexico, and opponents such as Senator Alfred Beveridge of Indiana roundly denounced the use of Spanish in classrooms and in the courts as evidence that *Nuevomexicanos* were ill-prepared for self-government and hence were unfit for entry into the Union. That year Hiram Hadley became superintendent. Hadley proved exceedingly intolerant of Spanish-language instruction, arguing that the 1891 school law had been misconstrued by his predecessors as providing for bilingual instruction. In fact, he insisted, the law merely allowed for teachers' *occasional* use of Spanish with students and with their parents. Hadley's successor, James Clark, similarly opposed bilingual education and convinced the Anglo-dominated state board to deny funding for Spanish-language textbooks. Clark further mandated that schools initiate so-called "Patriotic Days" to celebrate the "great men" in U.S history and to "Americanize" Spanish-speaking children.

To be certain, many *Nuevomexicanos* embraced the Americanizing project. But none . . . embraced the English-only policies of Hadley or Clark. In fact, those policies fueled a firestorm of protest from the *Nuevomexicano*-controlled territorial assembly, which hastily authorized the construction of a Spanish-American Normal School to revive bilingual education and to train bilingual teachers. Founded as a symbol of *Nuevomexicanos*' educational ambitions, the school unfortunately came to symbolize the neglect and dire reality of *Nuevomexicanos*' education.

In 1909, the territorial legislature passed a bill sponsored by L. Bradford Prince that called for the creation of the Spanish-American Normal School in El Rito. For more than thirty years, this school would stand as a symbol of *Nuevomexicano* education. Although it was created with the noble intention of training Spanish-speaking teachers to combat the lack of bilingual educators in rural districts, it was poorly funded and poorly attended, and in the 1920s was, effectively, transformed into a vocational school in which students handcrafted blankets, wood carvings, and furniture.

When Congress added an English-only provision into the statehood authorization bill, *Nuevomexicanos* responded by producing a constitution that guaranteed an education in Spanish to children "of Spanish descent." After sixty-two years of petitioning Congress, New Mexico entered the Union in 1912 as the nation's only officially bilingual state. Documents would be printed in both English and Spanish; there would be no English requirement to sit on a jury and, in the spirit of the 1891 school law, teachers would need to know Spanish in school districts where Spanish was the dominant language. But the mere fact of a bilingual constitution did not ensure the future of Spanish-language instruction. The struggle to retain Spanish in the schools, to legitimize its commercial and cultural value, would continue.

When Aurora Lucero stood before the conference of educators in 1911 and gave her eloquent defense of the Spanish language, she heralded the coming of an age in which *Nuevomexicanas* would play a growing role in education. She was at the forefront of a group of educated women who were entering the classroom and administration from the second decade of the twentieth century through the 1930s. Among her peers were women who pioneered, including Adelina Otero-Warren, Fabiola Cabeza de Baca, and Cleofas Jaramillo. Lucero would help to redefine language policy and instruction in the schools and contribute to what Sarah Deutsch and other scholars have called the "feminization of the Hispanic teaching force." In the process, she and her cohorts would invoke their *hispanidad* as a defense against attacks on their culture and language. The growth in numbers of women educators in New Mexico was rather remarkable after 1912, when women were granted the right to vote for and serve on school boards of education.

Lucero was the daughter of Antonio Lucero, a Spanish-language newspaper publisher and New Mexico's first secretary of state. She was educated at the Loretto Academy, Highlands University, and the University of Southern California. Although Lucero was a Spanish teacher for more than thirty years (1924–54) and briefly served as superintendent of education for San Miguel County (1925–27), there are few records of her public service. Nevertheless, three of her speeches from 1911 were published in local newspapers, and they offer a glimpse into the bilingual and Hispanist movement of which she and numerous men and women were a part.

Those speeches—in addition to defending bilingual instruction and denouncing English-only education—were replete with both Hispanist pride and U.S. patriotism. In one, for example, she embraced statehood as the culmination of a sixty-two-year struggle to enter what she called "the sisterhood of commonwealths of this mighty union." But she also warned her audience to beware threats to their language and heritage. She pronounced that "[t]o the south [of New Mexico], are sixty million people, all descended from the Spanish *Conquistadores*. To the north, are to be found the homes of at least ninety million of another people, nearly all of Anglo Saxon blood, speaking an entirely different language." New Mexico, she said, was the meeting ground between these two races, whose "amalgamation" was simply a question of time. Lucero predicted that "[t]he union of the calm, businesslike spirit of the Anglo-Saxon with the sanguine, chivalrous enthusiasm of the Castilian will be such a blending of all that is best in human nature . . . " Spanish and Anglo Saxon Americans were to be united in a single citizenship, under a single flag, and they were to acknowledge and respect one another's cultures, in her view.

But Lucero was keenly aware of the perils of statehood, for she knew there were those who believed one had to vanquish from the body politic all traces of culture and language that were not Anglo-Saxon. In a more immediate sense, she knew that most Anglo educators were determined to eliminate Spanish from the schools, the state constitution notwithstanding.

Though Lucero was a lifelong proponent of bilingualism, her prominence in this regard was eclipsed by that of her cousin, Adelina Otero-Warren. Born in 1881 into the same elite network of families, Adelina (or "Nina," as she preferred to be called) was educated at a private school in Saint Louis. Like Lucero, Otero met and married an Anglo American. She spent several years out of state before returning to New Mexico in 1912. Nina, however, became far more visible in politics. A leading suffragist and friend of Alice Paul, she immersed herself in political organizing and, in 1922, became the first New Mexico woman to run for Congress. Though she carried four of the five largest *Nuevomexicano* counties, she lost the election. By any measure, Nina Otero-Warren left the greatest imprint on the archival record of bilingual education in the state.

From 1917 to 1929, she was superintendent of education for Santa Fe County. In that capacity, and later as state supervisor for the literacy classes, she published numerous pamphlets and bulletins, and delivered speeches that promoted bilingual instruction. In one pamphlet, for example, she set forth a method for teaching English to non-English-speaking adults. She explained that teachers had to understand their students' cultural and historical background and make exercises that were culturally relevant to them. Earlier, in a speech, she noted that "Bilingualism has been called a problem rather than an asset." Schools had neglected their responsibility to educate Spanish-speaking students, she said,

> by giving to our children instructional materials that is New England in content and New England centered. By trying to get them to forget their language, their heritage; by sending to us experts to measure the child's ability by New England standards, a test which all of us would be fearful of taking.

To combat what she called the sense of "bewilderment" that Spanish-speaking students felt on entering school, Otero-Warren developed a curriculum that incorporated Spanish-language songs, local music, handicrafts, and Southwestern history. Otero-Warren is perhaps best remembered for her efforts to promote vocational training in traditional crafts, but her most enduring contribution to education was the "bilingual method" she developed to help students become proficient in Spanish as well as English. Considered rather "progressive" in its day, it involved teaching students to master material in English by way of graduated immersion, while separately teaching them proper Spanish grammar and composition. By 1938, this method was so widely implemented and lauded that the Taos County Teachers Association adopted a resolution calling for the direct method to be incorporated into the state's official curriculum. In justifying the resolution, County Superintendent Leonides Pacheco and County Supervisor Ruth C. Miller lamented that the "do not speak Spanish" doctrine of the schools had caused students to feel "ashamed of their language, their songs, their crafts and other home industries. We have many examples of the inhibitory effect of this method. . . . Spanish-speaking students should take pride in the ability to use correct Spanish as well as English, and they should be proud of their historical and cultural heritage."

Otero-Warren looked to Europe for her pedagogy and her roots. She was a fervent Hispanist and populist who believed—like her contemporary George Isadore Sánchez—that Spanish American identity cut across class boundaries, that even the poorest farmer could lay claim to a conquistadorial past. Indeed, that past was key to establishing primacy on the land, an equality with Anglo Americans and, especially, a white European heritage that would guarantee equality with other whites. . . . In 1930, for example, she pitched her literacy program to the Rockefeller Foundation thusly:

In the progress of American civilization we cannot overlook the fact
that the descendant of the Spanish Colonials (racially Spanish and
Mexican) is a native American. And yet the Spanish-American has
met the fate of all small Colonial Groups; namely, he has suffered
from the inability to compete economically or industrially with
the overwhelming odds of the standardized commercialism of this
country. In an effort to preserve the Spanish-American people and
their culture I feel this can best be accomplished through education.
Heretofore, there has been a neglect of the great opportunity to
incorporate the culture of these people—their arts and crafts—
in our educational work. Therefore, with a combination of
progressive American educational methods, together with the
stimulus to preserve their culture, the Spanish-Americans can
be put on a sound economic basis.

As part of her educational vision to both preserve *Nuevomexicanos'* traditions and uplift them economically, Otero-Warren proposed to document and
then incorporate Spanish colonial arts, crafts (old games, dances, religious
drama), and literature into a literacy curriculum. These "hidden resources,"
as she called them, were rapidly being lost through neglect, largely because
the Spanish language itself was viewed by many school officials as a barrier
and not a means to education. Lucero and Otero-Warren belong to a generation of *Nuevomexicana* educators whose story has yet to be told. Along with
Fabiola Cabeza de Baca and Cleofas Jaramillo, Lucero and Otero-Warren
became, effectively, brokers between *Nuevomexicano* and Anglo worlds. From
the 1930s through the 1950s, all of these women labored to conserve what
they saw as the most enduring vestiges of their identity: their language and
their folklore. Both inside the classroom and, often, in romantic and sometimes melancholy autobiographies, they also inserted their voices into discussions of *hispanidad*. Yet despite their advocacy of school reforms, the
"bilingual method" failed to extinguish the "do not speak Spanish" policy.
Indeed, the stigma associated with speaking Spanish in schools and public
realms only intensified with the passing years, even as Anglo Americans and
some *Nuevomexicanos* and *Nuevomexicanas*—including Otero-Warren herself—
reveled in their Spanish heritage.

Long after George Isadore Sánchez in 1940 spelled out the mournful state
of education among his "forgotten people," *Nuevomexicanos* remained on the

margins of the body politic, still yearning for full inclusion. It remains perhaps one of the greatest ironies of New Mexico's history that despite Anglo
Americans' professions of love for "all things Spanish," their adoration and
tourist dollars did not translate into civic, racial, or political equality for
"Spanish Americans." For, beneath the surface of Hispanophilia lurked its
alter ego: contempt. Contempt for those who presumed to assert some degree
of control over their own land, history, language, and destiny, and to attempt
to shift the parameters of "American" citizenship. But even as early as 1930,
Arthur Campa read the writing on the wall: neither Hispanophilia nor
hispanidad could redeem *Nuevomexicanos* from their marginal condition:

> That New Mexico remain[s] different with its Indians and with
> its somnolent Spanish villages is the desire of those in favor of
> the picturesque. That it develop along definite economic lines
> is the desire of those who see for the state a broader future than
> the mere amusement of tourists. That it can develop without
> sacrificing the heritage of a civilization that has been allowed
> to decay through neglect, isolation, and stagnation, is the ideal
> hope of many. (Pp. 197–205)

—*John M. Nieto-Phillips*

Beginning in the 1970s courts required schools to provide bilingual education. Since then it is part of both the federal and state rules schools must
follow.

CHAPTER TWO

New Mexico and World Events

Pancho Villa Raids New Mexico

While a young state, New Mexico became involved in world affairs. In 1916 a civil war raged in Mexico. Pancho Villa led one army in that war. He disliked the United States because it did not favor his side. The United States said Americans could not sell Villa guns or supplies. In an effort to gain these, he decided to raid the United States. As his target he chose Columbus, New Mexico, a town of 400 people.

In the early morning hours of March 9, 1916, Villa struck. His 500 men caught the town and the soldiers there by surprise. The raiders fanned out looking for guns and money. They set the town ablaze with gasoline. The fires, however, made the attackers perfect targets. American soldiers at Columbus fought back, driving off Villa's men. At sunrise the citizens of Columbus found much of their town in ashes. Villa had lost 90 men in the fight, while 10 citizens and 8 soldiers had died.

SELECTION FROM
Roadside New Mexico
A Guide to Historic Markers

Born Doroteo Arango in Chihuahua, Mexico, in 1878, Pancho Villa was a prominent figure in the Mexican Revolution. As a contender for the presidency of Mexico, Villa had grown resentful of the support the United States had given his opponent, Venustiano Carranza. The target of his revenge, the village of Columbus, was only thirteen years old in 1916. A small town born from a remote railroad camp, the settlement claimed 700 residents, 4 hotels, a bank, 3 restaurants, 2 barbershops, and an ice cream parlor.

Private Fred Griffin of the 13th Cavalry was posted as guard at Camp Furlong that morning. Griffin, seeing the Villistas approaching, shouted a warning to his fellow soldiers. Villa's men shot him in the stomach.

The siege began. Mexican mercenaries burned the Commercial Hotel, killing several inside. A gunshot killed the Columbus druggist, Charles C. Miller, as he ran from the Hoover Hotel to his drugstore to get rifles for defense. The rebels marauded down Broadway Avenue, burning much of the town. Soldiers at Camp Furlong grabbed their Springfield rifles and began to return fire. Although frightened and trapped inside her building, Susan Parks, the Columbus telephone operator, rang residents to warn them of the danger. The battle continued until just after dawn, when Villa and his men retreated to Mexico. (Pp. 341–42)

—David Pike

The United States now wanted to capture Villa. General John J. Pershing took 6,000 men into Mexico later in March. They advanced 400 miles into the country. But they never caught up with Villa. While chasing Villa, for the first time United States troops used trucks and airplanes in a foreign military operation. Pershing returned home empty handed. But New Mexicans would not forget that fateful morning in 1916 when the state had been invaded!

SELECTION FROM

Border Fury

A Picture Postcard Record of Mexico's Revolution and
U.S. War Preparedness, 1910–1917

The precise goal of the military campaign was muddled by [President] Wilson's uncertainties over the entire venture. He told the press that Pershing had been told to "Get Villa!" When reminded that such a chase might carry the U.S. Army beyond Mexico, even to South America, the president reduced the mission to the scattering of Villa's forces. Pancho Villa himself was no longer the target. [Nevertheless] the U.S. military command considered all attempts at diplomacy not relevant to the situation a waste of time. American territory had been attacked, and the army meant to punish the invaders. . . .

Pershing's disciplinary expedition of seasoned men crossed the international line into Mexico on March 15, 1916. Pershing commanded a supply train, plus companies of support troops and batteries of field artillery, some thirty-five miles south of Columbus, New Mexico. He ordered three flying columns of cavalry to the Papigochic region in pursuit of Villa. One of them proceeded with daring, if not official authorization, to batter a main party of Villistas at Guererro, the region's major town. He nearly captured Villa, who had been wounded in earlier combat but was evacuated as the Americans approached. This was the closest that the Pershing expedition ever came to catching its quarry. . . .

The United States did not want war with Mexico. Therefore, while diplomatic negotiations with Mexico intensified, the Wilson administration ordered Pershing to consolidate his forces near his headquarters and to restrict his army's forays into the countryside. By this time, it had also become apparent that U.S. government officials did not really care to capture Villa. Should they succeed, they wondered, what would they do with him? . . .

It has been argued that the expedition deliberately remained in Mexico so that the army could prepare itself for World War I. The mobilization and expedition permitted the army to test new equipment and to train personnel, to improve its command structure and modernize its supply and support services, for whenever and wherever they might be needed. Because of its Mexican venture, the U.S. Army finally became a twentieth-century fighting force, in large part due to Pancho Villa.

The Columbus raid gave the advocates of preparedness the wedge they needed to penetrate the national consciousness. . . . Villa tipped the balance toward military buildup. His assault not only propelled the Pershing expedition into Chihuahua but precipitated events that led to the mobilization along the border of the nation's entire national guard. It also advanced the National Defense Act of 1916, in which Congress agreed to budget an enlarged and modernized army. . . .

In the first place, the army became much more mobile, and supplies flowed more dependably as motor power replaced much animal power. The Columbus crisis provided an ideal testing ground, and myriad makes of trucks flowed to the border. Land vehicles passed the test; the experience with a new air force was more spectacular, if less successful. With motor vehicles the army learned what worked; with airplanes, it learned what did not. If the infant air force disappointed military expectations in Mexico, experimentation with mobile kitchens and hospitals, with sanitation measures and medicines held promise. The military also tried new signal corps wireless equipment and tested improved weaponry, such as machine guns and artillery. Based on their Mexican experience, cavalry officers recommended numerous changes, from the size and breed of their horses to the types of canteens carried by riders. Saddles, lariats, horseshoes, and rifles all received suggestions for improvements based on what occurred in Mexico. (Pp. 183–90)

— *Paul J. Vanderwood and Frank N. Samponaro*

The United States Goes to War

Shortly after pulling troops out of Mexico, the United States entered World War I. World War I had begun in 1914 in Europe. The Allies (Britain, France, Russia, and others) were on one side. Germany and nations friendly to it fought against them. At first the United States did not take sides. However, in 1917 that changed.

German actions brought the United States into the war. First, the Germans declared they would sink all ships sailing to Britain. This included American ships. Second, Americans learned of a German plan to give New Mexico, Arizona, and Texas to Mexico if it entered the war on the German side. An angry United States Congress declared war on Germany on April 6, 1917.

New Mexicans Do Their Share

New Mexicans joined their fellow Americans in supporting the war effort. Many young men rushed to join the army. When the University of New Mexico opened for its fall session in 1917, there were many fewer students. Seventy percent of the male students were missing, including the entire football team. The entire team had enlisted to fight. In all, some 17,251 New Mexicans served during the war.

Some of these fought in the 1918 battles in France that won the war. By the time the war ended, some 501 New Mexicans had died in military service. For a state with a small population, this was a high number. New Mexicans at home also aided the war effort. They bought more than their share of war bonds. To feed the army, farmers grew more wheat and potatoes. Ranchers raised more beef cattle. Likewise, wartime increased the demand for minerals. Miners produced more coal and copper, both minerals needed to fight a war. The efforts of New Mexicans helped the Allies win World War I on November 11, 1918.

A New Killer Claims Millions

Over 8 million soldiers died on the battlefields of World War I. The world had never seen such a slaughter. Indeed, people came to believe there would never be such a death toll ever again. However, just as the war drew to a close, a new, more deadly, killer appeared. And it too affected New Mexico. Doctors called this new killer the Spanish flu.

Scientists now believe it first appeared in Kansas in March 1918. From there it spread to Europe with American troops. Before long it had spread around the world, returning to the United States in the fall of 1918. Within a year the Spanish flu killed 21 million people. This was more than twice the number of soldiers killed in the battles of World War I. Of these flu deaths, 550,000 were Americans.

The Killer Strikes New Mexico
and the "Health Seekers" Arrive

The disease arrived in New Mexico in October 1918. It spread rapidly, killing more than 5,000 in the next few months. To fight the disease, officials banned public meetings. Police fined people for sneezing and spitting in public. Public schools became hospitals for the sick. To get paid, teachers in some towns worked as nurses. The flu struck hardest those between the ages of twenty and forty-five. Most flu victims in New Mexico lived in rural areas or small towns. However, to the relief of the world, in 1919, the flu epidemic ended as quickly as it started.

The flu epidemic passed, but the state attracted people suffering from other illnesses. People who had trouble breathing soon found New Mexico's climate helped them. Special facilities opened up for "health seekers." One such place was at Los Alamos, 20 miles northwest of Santa Fe. It was the site of a boy's ranch school until 1942.

SELECTION FROM
Los Alamos—The Ranch School Years, 1917–1943

On a late February day in 1918 a small towheaded boy, frail and racked with coughing, arrived in Santa Fe with his mother, his nurse, and his younger brother. They came by train from Kingman, Arizona, where they had been for several months, hoping in vain that the desert climate would improve the boy's fragile health. As they disembarked, they were approached by a tall, slender man in his mid-thirties, dressed in olive drab, wearing puttees, and a high-crowned Stetson hat. His blue eyes were set in a ruddy complexion, and pale thinning hair was barely visible under the large Stetson. The man's narrow face was coldly formal, but a hint of warmth flickered as he greeted them.

The man was Albert James Connell, director of the nine-month-old Los Alamos Ranch School, who had come the thirty miles from the ranch to welcome this new student, Lancellot Inglesby Pelly, and to assure Elizabeth Pelly that her son would be well taken care of at Los Alamos.

At the Santa Fe hotel that night, Lance was restless, recalling other family trips in search of a place where he would not be ill. In his eleven years he had attended school for only a few months. Most of his life had been spent in bed recovering from bronchitis, whooping cough, pneumonia or influenza—one illness after another. Some years he had a tutor, but studying tired him out, and then he would be sick and the tutor would be let go. He desperately wanted to run and play like other boys but, apart from his brothers, his only companions had been adults. Friends had suggested Los Alamos to his parents; they had heard it was designed to help just such boys as Lance.

The "outdoor school," as Los Alamos called itself, had opened the previous May with no classrooms or teachers, as envisioned by its founder, Ashley Pond Jr. He intended it to be a place where boys, rather than sitting at desks poring over textbooks, explored the countryside and helped run the ranch, with the area's archaeologists and forest rangers providing occasional informal instruction. In this manner, Pond believed sickly boys would gain health, strength, and self-confidence and in a few short months return to their regular schools. The school was slow in catching on, however, and Lance was one of the first to enroll on a full-time basis.

The Pellys were met the next morning by Director Connell and an older boy, Bill Rose, a member of Connell's Santa Fe Boy Scout troop who planned to enroll at Los Alamos the next fall. In the meantime, as a Scout who knew the ropes, Bill came to the ranch whenever he could to help new boys adjust to western life.

Their drive to the ranch that February took almost four hours over a rough dirt track called the Buckman Road, which led northwest from Santa Fe through steep arroyos and low-growing juniper and piñon trees, a few small brown adobe houses the only habitations. Dark evergreen-clad mountains capped with snow lined the eastern and western horizons, rising a mile above the dusty brown valley floor. It was strange country to Lance, accustomed as he was to the leafy green of Seattle, where his father Bernard was the British consul. Most unnerving was the descent into White Rock Canyon, where black basalt cliffs and boulder-covered slopes towered above the muddy Rio Grande and the railroad tracks running alongside it. They passed through Buckman, no more than a few ramshackle buildings and corrals beside the railroad, and crossed the river on a flimsy wooden span with no guardrails. On the other side, the road switch-backed steeply out of the canyon up what was called the Buckman Hill—a real "bugbear," Connell said when they stopped to let the radiator cool.

On the lower reaches of the Pajarito Plateau above the canyon, the piñon and juniper grew more thickly, interspersed with tall ponderosa pines. Turning north, they passed through broad canyons formed in volcanic tuff, the pale pink cliffs pocked with holes, some tiny, others enlarged by early Indian residents. When Mr. Connell talked about boys climbing cliffs and exploring the caves, the thought intrigued Lance but at the same time made him queasy. He had an unsettling mixture of happy anticipation and fear about this new place to which he was going.

Turning west up Los Alamos Canyon, the road ran along a small icy stream amid pine and fir, with snow deepening where the canyon narrowed. At a small garage and hay shed they parked the truck and climbed into a buckboard wagon, which Bill and Mr. Connell hitched to a horse. A steeply angled trail in a rocky side canyon soon brought them out on the upper level of the plateau. To the west a large barn and scattering of log buildings were visible amid the tall pines, and beyond these a mile or so the Jemez Mountains rose, their tops streaked with snow. To the north cattle grazed in wide fields. East toward Santa Fe they could see fields and low trees and then nothing at all, a vast emptiness and space where the plateau abruptly ended high above the river. Across the valley were the Sangre de Cristo Mountains, seeming almost close enough to touch, a dark blue wall against the eastern sky.

The horse stopped in front of a large two-story building of vertical logs, the main school building. Called the Big House, its broad façade was fronted on the east by a full-length portal where rocking chairs invited travelers to admire the magnificent view. They entered a large room whose softly glowing log walls were hung with patterned rugs and in the center of which stood a great freestanding stone fireplace. Before Lance could look around the room, however, Bill escorted them to the nearby guest cottage.

Like the other ranch buildings, the guest cottage was made of logs, its two small rooms furnished simply with iron bedsteads, rustic wooden furniture, wrought-iron fixtures, and Indian and Hispanic pottery and weavings. A welcoming fire blazed on the hearth, and late winter sun streamed through the windows. Shortly, a houseboy appeared with a tray of tea, milk, and cookies and in melodically accented English invited them to the Big House in an hour for midday dinner. The tense knot inside Lance's chest began to loosen a bit.

After his mother left, Lance moved into the Big House where, like the few other boys, he at first found the nights difficult, unaccustomed as he was to sleeping the year around in cold mountain air on a screened porch. The star-studded darkness seemed immense, and the nighttime silence made the boys uneasy. Nocturnal sounds sent shivers down their backs: the hooting of owls, the high-pitched yipping of coyotes, the eerie cries of mountain lions, and haunting howls of wolves. When the moon was full it washed the land in a ghostly silver light.

By day the high vault of deep blue sky that dominated the land held such clear air that it seemed one could see forever: north to where the mountains of southern Colorado spiked the horizon more than eighty miles away; south to the humped turtle shape of Sandia Mountain bordering Albuquerque; east to the Sangre de Cristos thirty miles away; west to where it seemed one could pick out individual trees on the Jemez ridges behind the ranch. In summer the mountains spawned towering dark thunderheads that announced their presence with loud alarms and blinding flashes. Rain sometimes came in great flooding downpours that filled arroyos with walls of brown water; at other times it sifted out of clouds in long gray streamers that evaporated before they reached the ground. Ashley Pond's daughter Peggy, an accomplished poet, captured well the dramatic views.

It was a vista that clutched at one's senses . . . the way great music
does. There was always movement going on in it—crescendos and

diminuendos of wind, fugues of light and shadow, the poise of a
bird balancing on invisible columns of air, the unfolding energy
of clouds, banners of rain that seemed to be carried through the
valley in ritual procession.

Winter's deep powdery snows were followed by skies of intense blue. Still
autumn days glowed like amber and painted golden patches on the mountains
and along the watercourses. In spring, strong winds scoured the land and filled
the air with stinging dust. A more dramatic setting for school life could scarcely
be imagined. This expansive world enveloped teenage boys accustomed to
horizons enclosed by buildings and smoky gray skies or to expanses of flat
green fields and tamer landscapes.

New Mexico was an exotic world for the schoolboys, but they gradually
came to know its ancient and historic landscapes. Spanish settlers arriving in
the 1600s had placed their towns and farms along the Rio Grande and its trib-
utaries, but the Jemez Mountains, lower and drier than the Sangres to the east,
attracted few settlers. West from the river that runs at the base of the Pajarito
Plateau, one passes from graveled canyon reaches of cottonwood and sage-
brush to progressively higher and cooler levels and finally onto the Jemez
slopes, where the tallest peak, sacred to the Indians, is Chicoma (or Tschicoma),
11,561 feet high.

The plateau and Jemez fostered layers of use and provided habitat for
black bear, mountain lion, wolf, deer, coyote, porcupine, badger, and raccoon,
whose tracks still threaded the slopes and canyons. Indians from nearby pueblos used the area's resources as they had for centuries, and descendants of
Spanish settlers hunted and farmed on the plateau. The nearest town of any
size was Española, twenty miles north beside the railroad tracks. On the plateau
a dozen or more homesteads were worked by mostly Hispanic families, who
grew corn and beans, grazed sheep and cattle, and periodically worked for the
Los Alamos Ranch, the Forest Service, or the area mines, patching together
a hard living from the land and a variety of seasonal jobs.

New Mexico's climate drew thousands of people who believed in the
health-giving qualities of high, dry air, especially for curing the scourge of
tuberculosis. Santa Fe had two sanatoriums: St. Vincent's, the oldest in New
Mexico, and Sunmount, an attractive facility developed in 1906 by Dr. Frank
Mera that drew people from around the country and was a center of cultural
life in Santa Fe. Like these health-seekers, Lance and the other boys thrived

on the plateau, just as Ashley Pond intended, roaming the mesas and mountain slopes on horseback. . . .

When Lance arrived in 1918, much of northern New Mexico seemed a remote corner of America. Trails and wagon tracks crossed the plateau, some leading into the mountains, where a few guest ranches and hot-springs spas operated periodically, but the best of these tracks were similar to the Buckman Road, hardly encouraging for travelers. Not surprisingly, the future of Los Alamos Ranch School depended on safer and more convenient access, and three years after Lance arrived the plateau became easier to reach. In 1921, the Culebra Hill road was built from the railroad crossing on the Rio Grande at Otowi to where the old road turned up Los Alamos Canyon, thus eliminating the bad stretch of road up Buckman Hill. To connect with this road, the school built a new section that switch-backed down Otowi Hill on the precipitous south face of Pueblo Canyon. While these new roads still twisted up steep grades and cliffs, causing many parents to be faint-hearted about visiting the school—more than one mother lay on the back seat with eyes tightly shut when transiting these sections—no longer was it necessary to use horse and wagon to reach the school in winter.

For all its isolation, however, the plateau was impacted by events in the larger world. For Pond and Connell, seeking to enroll boys from well-to-do urban families, the times were not auspicious. When unrest in Mexico spilled over the border in early 1916, the New Mexico National Guard was called up and American troops under General Pershing pursued Pancho Villa into Mexico. Easterners especially, knowing little about New Mexico, associated it with danger and violence. Then, in April 1917, the United States entered the Great War, and war fervor swept the nation. Before the conflict's end an influenza pandemic swept the world, killing hundreds of thousands in the United States, over five thousand in New Mexico alone. Given the national turmoil, it is not surprising that at first parents were slow to enroll their sons. The stream of visitors to New Mexico only temporarily slowed, however, and within a few years Los Alamos was fully subscribed.

It was both in spite of its isolation on the Pajarito Plateau and because of it that the Los Alamos Ranch School (LARS) thrived for twenty-five years. Set in beautiful and rugged country far from urban distractions, it was nevertheless a cosmopolitan community with strong ties to the nation's great urban centers. Its roots lay in the world of eastern boarding schools, in Progressive-era concerns about children and health, and in the intersecting paths of its founder, Ashley Pond Jr., and director, Albert J. Connell, on the Pajarito Plateau. Their roles in founding and shaping Los Alamos provide the essential threads from which the school's story is woven.

Unlike most boarding schools in the East, the Los Alamos Ranch School did not have a religious foundation nor was there an initial group of wealthy backers and contributors to the school. It was the inspiration of one man, Ashley Pond Jr., acting alone in response to the ill health he experienced in his childhood and young adult years. Albert Connell, as the school's only director, provided dedicated leadership and creative vision in the critical early years and developed the school's program. But the initial vision was Pond's: to combine the restorative powers of outdoor life in the New Mexico mountains with a loosely structured program of experiential learning in the Progressive mold then in vogue among American educators. It was, as an article in a Boston newspaper described it, a "school with Nature as a textbook." (Pp. 3–11)

—John D. Wirth and Linda Harvey Aldrich

CHAPTER THREE

Changes in the 1920s and 1930s

Artists Come to New Mexico

In the early 1900s many artists and writers were drawn to New Mexico. It began in 1898 with two painters, Bert G. Phillips and Ernest L. Blumenschein. They came to Taos by horse and wagon, seeking a place to settle and paint. In Taos they felt the effects of New Mexico's cultures. Blumenschein told Phillips, "This is what we are looking for. Let's go no farther." The two men saw in the Taos area "one great naked anatomy of majestic landscape, once tortured, now calm."

Other artists soon joined them. Some painted New Mexico's landscape. Others tried to capture on canvas the Indian and Hispanic cultures. In 1915 ten painters formed the famous Taos Society of Artists. The society arranged to show the artists' works around the nation. Likewise, numerous famous painters soon began an artists' colony in Santa Fe. Since then New Mexico has remained a center for the arts.

Writers Come to New Mexico

Writers also moved to Santa Fe and Taos. They came seeking a simpler way of life. They admired and wrote about the local cultures. Mary Austin arrived in Santa Fe in 1918 and founded the Santa Fe writers' colony. Her writings praised the Pueblo Indian culture. She contrasted this culture with the American culture and found the Pueblo culture superior.

Another famous writer who stayed for a while in Santa Fe was the novelist Willa Cather. While visiting at Mary Austin's home, Cather wrote most of her famous *Death Comes for the Archbishop*. Published in 1927,

Cather based this novel on the life of Archbishop Lamy and the French priests he brought to New Mexico.

Mabel Dodge Luhan, founder of the Taos writers' colony, arrived in that community in 1917. There she married Tony Luhan, a Taos Indian. To her roomy adobe home, Mabel Dodge Luhan invited writers to visit and work in Taos. Among these was a young New York poet named John Collier. Another was the famous British novelist D. H. Lawrence. The land of New Mexico affected Lawrence deeply. He later wrote, "In the magnificent fierce morning of New Mexico one sprang awake, a new part of the soul woke up suddenly, and the old world gave way to the new."

SELECTION FROM

Intimate Memories

The Autobiography of Mabel Dodge Luhan

Mabel was not impressed with the town of Taos, a frontier community of about 2,000 people: its center, a dilapidated green enclosed by crumbling adobe walls; its shops and stores bearing the marks of its status as a crossroads for traders. But the Pueblo Indians offer her the antithesis of all she has known and found wanting: both the materialistic world she grew up in and the chaotic world of new freedoms in which she had matured. Throughout her memoirs, she shows us how she has been impelled by a desire to devour the world in her frantic search to connect her solitary ego to something larger than itself. As described in *Edge of Taos Desert*, the Pueblos offer her—and potentially her fellow Americans—what no so-called advanced twentieth-century society was able to: a model of a fully integrated society that is achieved through an intimate connection between individual and community, work and living space, play and art. . . .

Swept clean of the waste and sickness of civilization by New Mexico's "undomesticated" landscape, where life is reduced to its "bare essentials," Luhan shows in *Edge of Taos Desert* how her newly adopted home and lover influence the rebirth of her imagination. In fact, it was in New Mexico that Luhan found her voice as a writer, just as other strong women, such as Mary Austin, Willa Cather, and Georgia O'Keeffe, were drawn to its allure as a seemingly masterless frontier in which they could inscribe an original, creative vision. (Pp. xv–xvii)

— Lois Palken Rudnick

Interest in Local Arts and Crafts Renewed

Indian and Hispanic arts and crafts gained new appreciation. The 1920s witnessed the revival of superb pottery making. Pueblo Indians in particular made fine pottery. The most famous potter was Maria Martínez of San Ildefonso Pueblo. Maria rediscovered a forgotten, thousand-year-old method of making pottery. She shaped and fired the pots, while her husband Julian Martínez and other men painted designs on the pots. Maria's black-on-black pottery eventually sold in elegant shops along Fifth Avenue in New York City.

The revival of traditional Pueblo pottery in the 1920s was also followed by many changes and innovations to the tradition.

SELECTION FROM

Fourteen Families in Pueblo Pottery

Tradition itself is constantly being reinvented in Pueblo pottery. The distinctive carved pottery of Santa Clara and San Ildefonso was first made as recently as the 1920s. The sgraffito technique [a technique used to decorate ceramics in which the top layer has patterns scratched into it, revealing the different-colored layer beneath] is old to other parts of the world but very new to Pueblo pottery, begun by Popovi-Da and Tony Da at San Ildefonso in the mid-to-late 1960s and carried to a pinnacle by Joseph Lonewolf and his family in the very early 1970s. In the 1990s potters from virtually every pueblo employ the sgraffito technique, and it is especially popular at Santa Clara. Using the technique on their slip-cast ware, Jemez, San Ildefonso, Acoma, and Laguna potters have created a whole new tourist market.

The black-on-black pottery made popular by Maria and Julian Martínez of San Ildefonso Pueblo was first made in the late teens of the twentieth century. The storyteller figures of Cochiti, though related to a figurative tradition of the latter part of the 1800s, were not made until the 1960s—spearheaded by Helen Cordero.

Hopi, Hopi/Tewa, and Zia potters . . . have carried on traditions that began centuries ago in their villages. But as commercialism becomes more prevalent in these villages, styles and tastes may change. Acoma Pueblo still keeps old stylistic traditions alive, but the electric kiln has all but supplanted the traditional sheep-manure firing.

The function of pottery has changed too—once made to be of practical use, it is now perceived as an art object. Service pottery and ceremonial pottery for personal and village use continue to be made today, and pottery is still traded among the pueblos as it has been for centuries. The difference in today's pottery manufacture is the Anglo desire to own unique and exceptional pieces. This has created divisions among potters and collectors alike. (Pp. xiii–xiv)

— *Rick Dillingham*

Navajo weavers also returned to older ways of making rugs. After 1890 they had stopped putting native designs into their rugs. At the urging of traders and collectors, weavers again began using native designs. Weavers also again used local dyes made from plants, fruits, and berries. Also in the 1920s, Navajo and Pueblo silversmiths continued to make fine jewelry.

SELECTION FROM
Diné
A History of the Navajos

During this period a Diné woman known to the general public simply as Elle of Ganado became an important symbol of Navajo weaving. An employee of the Fred Harvey Company from 1903 to 1923, Asdzáá Lichii ("Red Woman") was based at the Alvarado Hotel in Albuquerque. She also traveled widely on the Santa Fe Railway to demonstrate the beauty of Diné weaving, journeying to the Hopi House at the Grand Canyon, the Panama-Pacific International Exposition in San Francisco, and various shows in Chicago. One of most publicized moments came when she wove a red, white, and blue rug in the form of an honorary membership card for the Commercial Club of Albuquerque that she presented to President Theodore Roosevelt. A photogenic person as well as a gifted weaver, Elle of Ganado was photographed frequently by the Harvey Company, and that image was used to promote travel on the Santa Fe Railway and stays at the Harvey Houses. . . . The Harvey Company helped expand popular knowledge about and sales of Diné weaving. Herman Schweitzer, manager of the company's "Indian Department," worked closely over thee decades with J. L. Hubbell of Ganado to market Navajo rugs. Schweitzer purchased 1,657 textiles from Hubbell in 1908, and 2,094 in the following year; Hubbell's biographer, Martha Blue, contends that Hubbell's standing among the Navajos made it possible for the Santa Fe Railway to recruit Elle of Ganado and other Diné to work for the railroad company.

. . . Traders had an important if unintended effect on Navajo life by altering work and trade patterns and practices. As weaving became more marketable, it became less an item of trade and more an item to be purchased by outsiders, which introduced cash into the equation. At the same time, Navajos also began the transition from wearing blankets of their own manufacture to blankets made elsewhere. The growth of the Pendleton Mills from Oregon and the greater availability of their fine blankets helped expedite this change, together with the greater availability of western clothing. (P. 131)

—Peter Iverson

Local Hispanic weaving also revived. At Chimayó weavers once again produced handspun, vegetable-dyed blankets like their ancestors had made during the century before. The demand for quality Chimayó blankets grew. Wool embroidery by Hispanic women was also valued as art worth saving. Fashioned with long stitches, the embroideries featured plant and animal forms. The most popular embroideries were *colchas* (bedspreads) and *sabinillas* (altar cloths).

SELECTION FROM
The Lore of New Mexico

Chimayó's commerce was stimulated by its status as a pilgrimage center. In 1916, Paul A. F. Walter described it as "a New Mexico Lourdes" and gave the following version of the *Santuario* legend:

It was some years after the Chimayó rebellion in 1837, that a priest came to the settlements on the upper Santa Cruz, which are known under the collective name of Chimayó. He ministered to the people who were without a church, and after a while asked them to build a chapel on a spot he had selected. But the people were too indifferent and refused to heed the admonition. One day the priest disappeared and the next morning, from a cottonwood tree that stood on the spot designated by the priest for a chapel, there protruded a foot. The people were so impressed with the miracle that they built the chapel and made it the most beautiful church in all of New Mexico.

El Santuario was in danger of being dismantled in 1929, when three members of the Cháves family, among them María de los Angeles Cháves, Bernardo Abeyta's granddaughter, could no longer afford their property. Members of the Society for the Preservation and Restoration of New Mexico Mission Churches and what was then known as the Society for the Revival of Spanish Arts, notably Santa Feans E. Dana Johnson, John Gaw Meem, Alice Corbin Henderson, Frank Applegate, and Mary Austin, arranged for an anonymous donation, which was given to Don José Cháves by Archbishop Albert T. Daeger on October 15, 1929, the same day that official incorporation papers for the Spanish Colonial Arts Society were signed. Writer Mary Austin "was able to find a Catholic benefactor who made possible the purchase of the building and its contents, to be held in trust by the Church for worship and as a religious museum, intact, and no alterations to be made in it without our consent." (P. 62)

—Marta Weigle and Peter White

The paintings and carvings of santeros also gained new respect. Whole families revived the almost lost art of woodcarving. One such family was the José Dolores López family of Cordova, a village near Chimayó. The revival of Hispanic arts and crafts further led to new interest in other art forms. Efforts began at the University of New Mexico to preserve New Mexican folk dramas and folk music.

SELECTION FROM

Tradiciones Nuevomexicanas
Hispano Arts and Culture of New Mexico

In the 1920s, the Taos and Santa Fe art colonies were established by Anglo-American artists who had recently moved to New Mexico, attracted by the climate and exotic local cultures. They sometimes painted Hispanos and santos into their own works, but only as elements of local color. In no way did local painting styles or subject matter influence their own styles. Several artists studied and collected the old santos. Frank Applegate is credited with approaching the old *retablos* and *bultos* as genuine works of religious art rather than as curios. He became one of the most active buyers of Spanish colonial art, and together with Mary Austin, founded the Spanish Colonial Arts Society in 1929. Since that time, the Society has been responsible for the rescue, restoration, and collecting of numerous works of religious art, from small pieces to an entire church (the *Santuario* at Chimayó). It continues today to promote and encourage the research and production of traditional arts of New Mexico and to host the annual Spanish Market, a yearly outdoor exhibit and the most important exhibit of traditional *Nuevomexicano* art in New Mexico. . . .

The artisans themselves had only a little familiarity with their artistic heritage after their churches had been redecorated in European styles by Bishop Lamy's French and Italian priests. Yet these artisans were looking for a way to avoid the migrant farm circuit and make ends meet at home. Thus did José Dolores López (1868–1937) of Córdova agree to carve nontraditional items such as lazy susans, record racks, and screen doors in addition to the more traditional pieces. José Dolores López was the son of Nasario López (who may have worked with José Rafael Aragón), father of George López, and grandfather of Gloria López Córdova, Sabinita López Ortiz, and Eluid Martínez, all excellent carvers.

The most significant and long-lasting result of this interaction was that López stopped painting his carvings as suggested by Applegate and Austin, who regularly sold his work in Santa Fe. They found the house paints he used too bright and bold. Thus began the unique Córdova School of carving, which is distinguished from all other work by its lack of paint, and its reliance on detailed incising and chip carving to delineate the features of each piece. By influencing López's output and style, Applegate and Austin were able to combine his artistic inclinations with the tastes of the Santa Fe Anglo market. In following their advice, López found a market niche created for him, and in turn he created a new style of woodcarving that was closer to contemporary Western art than authentic Spanish colonial works of New Mexico. Interestingly, it was only at the suggestion of Applegate and Austin that López began carving santos late in life.

José Dolores López is probably the most documented *santero* of New Mexico. Born in 1868, he began as a carpenter and filigree jeweler. His unique and intricate chip-carved style also was introduced by Anglo-Americans who had seen chip-carved pieces in Switzerland. Today, it is the signature style of the villages of Córdova and Chimayó.

As *hermano mayor* of his *cofradía* and *sacristán* of the chapel at Córdova, López came under some criticism from his neighbors for selling religious images to Anglo Protestants. A friend of the Lópezes said:

> I remember talking to José Dolores . . . before he died. He told me that the santos he was making weren't from the heart, they weren't religious, but "God won't mind if I make enough money to live. God is happy for anybody who has the initiative to work his own way. This way was good," José Dolores said, "because you were working for yourself."

He didn't call them santos, but *monos*, meaning dolls or figures, especially deformed ones. The controversy over selling religious images to nonbelievers, or for money, continues today. Some santeros feel it is a sin to sell santos to nonbelievers, and will sell only secular items to the general public. Others, like late twentieth-century *santero* Charles Carrillo, believe a santo is not a holy object until it has been blessed. (Pp. 40–45)

—Mary Montaño

SELECTION FROM
Tradiciones Nuevomexicanas
Hispano Arts and Culture of New Mexico

The first half of the twentieth century also saw a large increase in audiences for both traditional and popular Hispanic music, partially as a result of growing activity in the Southwest by the recording industry, and partially as a result of traditional music performances at festivals and other intercultural public events in the Southwest, and subsequently around the nation. Commercial recording companies set up shop in southern Texas in the 1930s to record local musicians, thus shining a spotlight on musical genres that had never before been heard outside the Southwest. Several types of music that developed in southern Texas greatly influenced New Mexico musicians, including *música norteña* (an instrumental dance music of the working class characterized by the use of the button accordion and known also as Mexican-Texan *conjunto* or *conjunto norteño*), *ranchera* (Mexican country), and *La Coda Chicano* (Chicano Wave—a fusion of Mex-Tex ranchero, American jazz, and rock, popular in the 1970s). Other genres partially assimilated in New Mexico include Latin rock and *música tropical*, or *salsa*, from Latin America and other Hispanic population centers within the United States, such as New York, Los Angeles, Miami, and Chicago.

Also highly popular in the Southwest are mariachi bands and the *orquesta típica*, both developed in Mexico from the same nineteenth-century ensemble type. *Orquesta típica* is an ensemble built around the violin, always with one or more guitars and occasionally a psaltery (an instrument comprised of a flat soundboard over which strings are stretched). When this genre migrated to the Southwest in the 1920s, other instruments were added as available. Today José Pablo Garcia's *orquesta típica* of Las Vegas, New Mexico, is one of the best known in the state.

The mariachi band developed as a folk tradition in rural Mexico. It was comprised entirely of stringed instruments, the most authentic and the earliest combination being the violin, *vihuela*, and harp. When adopted in Mexico's urban areas and featured on radio broadcasts in the 1930s, the trumpet replaced the harp so that it could be more easily heard over the radio. Its success was such that the "trumpet mariachi" became Mexico's unofficial national ensemble. In New Mexico, mariachi music did not catch on until it was heard on the radio and in Mexican films during the 1930s and 1940s, and with the arrival of more and more Mexican immigrants into the area since the 1950s. Local musicians adopted its style and New Mexicans made it highly popular, particularly for public events. Today, Mexican-American mariachi bands experiment with instrumentation by adding conga drums and accordions, for example, and by the addition of female musicians. Mariachi music is celebrated every July in Albuquerque at the Mariachi Spectacular, which invites bands from the United States and Latin America to interact with students and enthusiasts in a weeklong series of classes, discussions, rehearsals, and public performances. . . .

The Sánchez Family, headed by Alberto "Al Hurricane" Sánchez, also has gained considerable fame in New Mexico and the Southwest in the area of popular and rock music. In the 1950s, Al Hurricane and his brothers—Mauricio,

"Tiny Morrie," and Gabriel, "Baby Gaby"—succeeded in transposing the *ranchera* tradition into a local style that included trumpet and saxophone arrangements known as the "Albuquerque sound." They performed original songs, plus the occasional *corrido* and old New Mexico tunes, bringing those tunes to a larger audience. The family's current musical focus has been on the next generation, including the internationally popular "Lorenzo Antonio" and five Sánchez girls, who have formed a highly profitable, internationally popular Latin rock group called Sparx. It is interesting that this pop-oriented group has recorded its own engaging, high-energy versions of *corridos* and even "*La Rana*" without compromising or obscuring its traditional origins.

With the increasing accessibility of recording technology, community bands and singers throughout New Mexico began producing cassettes and later, compact discs, of their music for distribution primarily in New Mexico. It was only a matter of time before an organization dedicated to recognizing and encouraging New Mexico Hispanic music of all genres would be established. The New Mexico Hispano Music Association held its first annual awards ceremony in Santa Fe in 1991. Since then, the association has presented awards to individual performers, composers, dance bands specializing in popular and traditional music, and lifetime achievement awards. While the New Mexico Hispano Music Association was initially designed for popular, *ranchera*, rock, and *norteño* music, organizers added a folk category not long after its founding, due to popular demand. (Pp. 175–83)

—*Mary Montaño*

Pueblo Indians Gain Rights

Also in the 1920s, New Mexico's Pueblo peoples entered politics. They united for the first time since the Pueblo Revolt of 1680. At issue was their land. Some individual Indians had sold tribal lands to non-Indians. In 1913, the United States Supreme Court said that was illegal. But many non-Indians continued to live on the Pueblo land. They claimed they owned the land because they had paid for it.

The issue of Pueblo land ownership had to do with the Pueblos' legal status as Indian tribes in the eyes of the federal government.

SELECTION FROM
New Mexico Government, THIRD EDITION

Pueblo is a Spanish word that, in this instance, means "village." Each of the nineteen New Mexico pueblos is a recognized Indian tribe. Although their manner of living, religious practices, and culture may seem to the outsider to be the same, they are often very different. And their languages are often very different, too. Pueblo languages fall into three linguistic groupings: Tanoan (with three subgroupings, Tiwa, Tewa, and Towa); Keres; and Zuni, a language unique to that pueblo alone.

Present-day New Mexico pueblos are located in six counties. In the north, Taos Pueblo and Picuris Pueblo, both Tiwa-speaking, are located in Taos County; there are six Tewa-speaking pueblos (San Juan, Santa Clara, San Ildefonso, Nambé, Pojoaque, and Tesuque) in Rio Arriba County. To the south there are seven pueblos in Sandoval County (the five Keres-speaking pueblos of Cochiti, Santo Domingo, San Felipe, Santa Ana, and Zia; Towa-speaking Jemez Pueblo; and Tiwa-speaking Sandia Pueblo). Tiwa-speaking Isleta Pueblo is located just south of Albuquerque in Bernalillo County. To the west, in Valencia County, are the Keres-speaking pueblos of Laguna and Acoma. Zuni Pueblo is farther west, in McKinley County.

When New Mexico was a territory of the United States, the Pueblos were not considered by federal law to be Indians, because they were said to be too settled and "civilized." Thus, for example, their lands were not protected by federal law on the same basis as the lands of other tribes, nor were the Pueblos entitled to the same services that the federal government provided to other tribes. Then in 1913, the U.S. Supreme Court declared that the pueblos were recognized Indian tribes, after all. In the case of *United States v. Sandoval*, the Court said:

> The people of the Pueblos, although sedentary rather than
> nomadic in their inclinations and disposed to peace and industry,
> are nevertheless Indians in race, customs, and domestic government,
> always living in separate and isolated communities, adhering to
> primitive modes of life, largely influenced by superstition and
> fetishism, and chiefly governed according to the crude customs
> inherited from their ancestors. They are essentially a simple,
> uninformed, and inferior people.

Thus, in highly patronizing, even racist, words were the rights of the Pueblo Indians upheld! After that court decision, the pueblos were entitled to the same federal protection of their lands and the same federal services provided for other Indian tribes throughout the United States. (Pp. 195–96)

—*Fred R. Harris and LaDonna Harris*

In 1922 United States Senator Holm O. Bursum of New Mexico tried to settle the land question. He proposed what was called the "Bursum Bill" to Congress. This bill would have let non-Indians keep the land they had bought. Pueblo leaders knew nothing of this bill, but friends of theirs did. Writers and artists rallied to their cause. Poet John Collier traveled with Tony Luhan from pueblo to pueblo. At each stop they sounded the alarm. The Pueblo leaders united to fight Bursum's bill. Some of them traveled to Washington, D.C., to argue for their land.

The Indians succeeded. Bursum's bill was defeated and replaced by another. In 1924 this became the Pueblo Lands Act. This law once and for all recognized the land rights of the Pueblo peoples. It returned the sold lands to the Pueblos. It outlined ways to get non-Indians off Indian lands and how they would be paid. Also in 1924 Congress went farther. It passed another law giving citizenship to Indians born in the United States. (Spain and Mexico had regarded the Indians as citizens.) However, Arizona and New Mexico did not grant Indians the right to vote until 1948.

SELECTION FROM
New Mexico Government, THIRD EDITION

Dual citizenship of American Indians who are members of tribes means that, like all American citizens, they are: 1) citizens of the United States (as a result of which, by operation of the Fourteenth Amendment to the Constitution, they are citizens of the states where they reside, too); and 2) they are also citizens of the tribes of which they are members. Because of treaties, constitutional provisions, acts of Congress, and decisions of the federal courts and the Supreme Court, the tribal governments of American Indians, unlike the private organizations of other ethnic groups such as the League of United Latin American Citizens or the National Association for the Advancement of Colored People, are units of government.

Thus our American "federal system" of shared sovereignty is not just composed of federal, state, and local governments. It is made up of federal, state, local, and *tribal* governments. . . .

Dual entitlement means that (again, because of treaties, constitutional provisions, acts of Congress, and decisions of the federal courts and the U.S. Supreme Court) American Indians receive the same services as other citizens and are also entitled to certain additional services, such as health services, because they are American Indians (but they do not receive individual federal payments as Indians, as some people may think).

Indians have made considerable progress in recent times. There are now, for example, more than ten thousand American Indian professionals—lawyers, doctors, accountants, engineers, and others. Indians are no longer the very poorest Americans. But as a group, they are still far behind white America; the percentage of families living below the poverty line is more than twice that for the rest of the population, and the percentage of those who have completed four years of college is less than half that for the total population. (P. 188)

—*Fred R. Harris and LaDonna Harris*

CHAPTER FOUR

The Great Depression

The Great Depression Begins

Many Americans viewed the 1920s as one of the most prosperous decades in history. In 1929, however, all that changed. In that year the stock market crashed, and hard times followed. The stock market crash set off a chain of events. These events led the United States deeper and deeper into depression.

Depression is a term used to describe an extremely troubled economy. A depression is a time when many people are out of work. As a result, people buy fewer goods because they have less money. Less buying, in turn, leads to lower prices. Businesses lose money and lay off more workers. The spiral downward continues, leading to more workers losing their jobs and to still less buying of goods. The depression of the 1930s is called the Great Depression. This is because it was the worst depression in United States history, and it lasted for over ten years.

Civilian Conservation Corps

To help provide jobs, the U.S. government set up work programs. One was the Civilian Conservation Corps. Many young men signed up for the Civilian Conservation Corps in New Mexico. They worked hard. Their results were astounding. A record of their achievements hangs on the wall of the state capitol building. It has hung there since 1992. Here is what it says:

US CCC
"Spirit of the CCC" 1933–1942
plaque in the state capitol building in Santa Fe,
dedicated on the 59th Anniversary of the
Founding of the CCC, March 31, 1992
Civilian Conservation Corps

During the Great Depression of the 1930s when financial disaster, environmental ruin, 25 percent unemployment, and hunger stalked this land, 54,500 Civilian Conservation Corps (CCC) members served in New Mexico. They were part of the 3.5 million members, including 225,000 veterans in 4,500 camps throughout the nation. These members replenished our forests, built state and national parks, thousands of lakes, public buildings, dams, reservoirs, fish hatcheries, wildlife refuges, phone lines, roads, and many other needed projects too numerous to mention. They restored Civil War battlefields, thousands of historic structures, and millions of Dust Bowl acres in America's heartland.

In New Mexico, CCC members constructed the Bosque Del Apache Wildlife Refuge, Bandelier National Monument, the Southwest regional headquarters building for the National Park Service in Santa Fe, and State parks including Hyde Park, River Park, Conchas, Elephant Butte, and Bottomless Lakes Park. They made major improvements in Carlsbad Caverns, built 795 bridges, 658 dams and reservoirs, wells, many miles of roads, trails and fences, planted six million trees, restored Chaco Canyon Ruins, and reseeded thousands of acres of grazing land.

When WWII began, ex-CCC members made up about 20 percent of America's armed forces. Their dead, which numbered in the tens of thousands, attest to their contributions to the cause of freedom. General George C. Marshall, Army Chief of Staff, later credited their training in the CCC as a major factor in America winning WWII.

This tribute to the members of the Civilian Conservation Corps was requested by Senate Joint Memorial 16 of the 37th Legislature Second Session, 1986. It was brought to reality by the joint efforts of the Legislative Council and the New Mexico Roadrunner Chapter #14 of the National Association of the Civilian Conservation Corps Alumni (NACCCA).

New Mexico's Farmers Are Hard Hit

Across the nation farmers and ranchers were hurt by the depression. In New Mexico dry farmers were hardest hit. They suffered from a lack of rainfall. Indeed, New Mexico was part of a region called the Dust Bowl. The Dust Bowl lacked moisture. It was also hit by high winds. From Oklahoma to eastern New Mexico the winds picked up the dry land. The winds blew away great clouds of topsoil. Thick dust filled the air. People could not see more than a foot or two in any direction. Dust buried and killed entire crops.

Soon farmers lost their land. Some of them then became tenant farmers. They farmed land that was owned by someone else. Tenant farmers paid rent in crops or money to the land owners. Other farmers who lost their land became migrant workers. They traveled from place to place. They harvested crops grown by someone else. Still other farmers who lost their land could find no work.

One writer remembers discovering Pie Town, New Mexico, a small town affected by the depression.

SELECTION FROM

Pie Town Woman

Pie Town. Seeing the name on the highway sign, I put my foot on the brake and slowed down. The name made me think of potluck suppers, Sunday school, Main Street parades and moms who stay at home to bake bread and drive their kids to piano lessons after school. The name conjured up a past innocence, a destiny of family and community roots, a timeless place.

I remembered the name Pie Town, vaguely, from a 1941 *U.S. Camera* article with photographs by Russell Lee. Russell Lee worked for the history division of the Farm Security Administration, the FSA, from 1936 to 1942. He and his wife Jean traveled eleven months of the year photographing the effects of the New Deal agricultural policies on people who had suffered through the Depression and Dust Bowl. When the Lees arrived in Pie Town in mid-April, 1940, they were charmed by the struggles and spirit of the remote New Mexican town with the whimsical name. They decided to take extra time and record what they saw.

When I drove into Pie Town that morning, I could not recall many specific images. All I knew was that Lee had succeeded in making a set of pictures that typified the struggles of families to eke out a living in the difficult years between the Depression and World War II. I did remember a photograph of a woman looking proudly at one of her jars of canned goods. . . .

That morning I could well have missed Pie Town altogether. A sip of coffee at the wrong time and I might not have paid attention to the few buildings that lined the highway—the Break 21 Café, a tiny post office with a handmade sign, and a couple of small wooden houses festooned with discarded appliances and parts from rusty pickups. Curious, I left the highway and drove through the oldest part of Pie Town, along a dirt road that had been the main highway before a bypass was paved in 1957. There were no traffic lights. I stopped at the only stop sign, but it seemed more of a formality than a necessity. A three-legged dog eyed me without interest and hopped across the intersection diagonally.

Most houses were unpainted and boarded up. A few homes were occupied and landscaped with gardens of blue and purple bottles set on fence posts. In 1935, about three hundred families lived in Pie Town. Today, fewer than a hundred residents live within a twenty-mile radius. A small, white, clapboard rectangular building had a sign reading "Community Center," but it was closed. Nearby was a small park with seesaws, swings, and a basketball hoop, but it was empty. Both the Baptist and Latter-day Saints churches looked in good condition and offered regular services but surely neither could boast a large congregation, guessing from the size of the town.

I stopped in the café for a cup of coffee and chatted with Lester Jackson, an ex-Marine who had bought the place with his wife Emily, in February 1976. He was a cheerful, stocky man with tattoos on both arms, short gray hair and a small mustache. He told me he had moved to Pie Town after four tours of duty in Vietnam, opened the café and started baking pies. He cut me a generous slice of his apple pie, which was flaky and delicious. A plate on the wall indicated that the Jacksons had made 17,718 pies since they bought the place.

When I complimented his pie, Lester reached under the counter and brought up a well-worn copy of a 1983 article from the *Albuquerque Journal*. A photo showed Lester standing behind Jones, the previous town pie maker. Though Lester was a relative newcomer to town, he showed it to me with the pleasure of a man who drew sustenance from a long-simmering and rich history that now included him. (Pp. 43–45)

—Joan Myers

Ranchers Also Suffer

On a ranch near Las Vegas, young Fabiola Cabeza de Baca witnessed the worst of the Dust Bowl. Day after day the wind blew. She recalled, "The whole world around us was a thick cloud of dust." The dust seeped into her father's ranch house. It was everywhere. In the mornings she could see her shape imprinted in the dust on her sheets. On some days Fabiola reported she did not see the sun.

She did not go outside for fear of breathing nothing but dust. She saw the land become desolate as grass disappeared. Without grass, it became more difficult for cattle to survive. Finally, her father, like many other ranchers, had to sell his cattle and leave the land, such being the effect of three years without rain.

SELECTION FROM

We Fed Them Cactus

Papá built up his herd according to the capacity of his land, but droughts came again in 1933. There was no rain from the fall of 1932 until the third of May, 1935 and the drought was not broken until that winter, when a foot of snow covered the Ceja and the Llano.

The land, between the years 1932 and 1935, became a dust bowl. The droughts, erosion of the land, the unprotected soil and overgrazing of pastures had no power over the winds. The winds blew and the land became desolate and abandoned. Gradually the grass and other vegetation disappeared and the stock began to perish. There was not a day of respite from the wind. The houses were no protection against it. In the mornings upon rising from bed, one's body was imprinted on the sheets which were covered with sand. One no longer breathed pure air, and continuous coughing indicated that one's lungs were permeated with the fine sand. One forgot how it felt to touch a smooth surface or a clean dish; how food without grit tasted, and how clear water may have appeared. The whole world around us was a thick cloud of dust. The sun was invisible and one would scarcely venture into the outdoors for fear of breathing the foul grit.

The winds blew all day and they blew all night, until every plant which had survived was covered by hills of sand. . . .

Papá kept on feeding his cattle, but the day came when his purse became empty and he could no longer buy feed. He became disillusioned and as quickly lost the strength to fight. . . .

The government started buying the cattle and killing off those which were too poor to move. Papá's cattle were in good condition, but he did not know how long they could survive, so along with other cattlemen he had to sell. He could not take it and he became ill of an illness from which he never recovered. For the cows that were killed, he was paid twelve dollars per head; for those that were in good shape he received eighteen and the calves brought six dollars.

Papá was past sixty and he knew it would be many years before the land would come back; he knew he could not start again.

The land which he loved had sucked the last bit of strength which so long had kept him enduring failures and sometimes successes but never of one tenor. Life so cruel and at times so sweet is a continuous struggle for existence—yet one so uncertain of what is beyond fights and fights for survival. One has not lived who has not experienced reverses. Papá had a full life.

He is gone, but the land which he loved is there. It has come back. The grass is growing again and those living on his land are wiser. They are following practices of soil and water conservation which were not available to Papá. But each generation must profit by the trials and errors of those before them; otherwise, everything would perish. (Pp. 171–78)

—Fabiola Cabeza de Baca

Early in the depression help for those in need came from several sources. Churches did charity work. Local offices for the needy also provided some help. However, as things got worse, local efforts were not enough. As a result, major efforts to help the poor and jobless shifted in 1933 to the national government.

Needy New Mexicans Find Help

Formal relief, meaning the government's caring for people in need, was part of a new program. This program was called the New Deal. The New Deal was the name given to the programs of President Franklin D. Roosevelt. Roosevelt won election as president in 1932. Taking office in 1933, he sent New Deal relief programs to Congress. Congress quickly passed the acts that Roosevelt wanted.

New Mexicans welcomed these programs. In some counties more than half the people enrolled in these programs by 1935. This was most common in the eastern counties. There, drought and dust storms made ranching and farming difficult.

Some New Deal programs put people to work. The Works Progress Administration (WPA) put people to work in many kinds of jobs. Writers, artists, and musicians worked for the WPA. Others built schools and other public buildings, such as libraries and post offices. Many of these schools and buildings are still used by the public today. By 1936 more than 13,000 New Mexicans had found jobs through the WPA.

New Deal Programs Help Young People

Two other New Deal programs produced jobs for New Mexicans as well. The first was the Civilian Conservation Corps (CCC) (See page 55). The second was the National Youth Administration (NYA). Both programs were designed to help young people.

The CCC employed young men between the ages of 18 and 25. These young men worked in soil conservation projects. They worked in forest improvement projects. They lived in camps. Part of what they earned each month went directly to their families. A CCC branch for young Indian men employed them in flood control and irrigation projects. This CCC branch helped increase farm production on Pueblo lands.

The NYA, the second program, emphasized job training. Those trained under the NYA received wages for their training. In Clayton, for example, young people learned skills in woodworking, metal work, adobe work, and weaving. The youth of Clayton then helped build their school. The NYA trained many people. The country was glad to have these skilled workers when the Second World War began.

The Depression Changes Politics

New Mexico politics changed in the 1930s. Until then, the Republican party had controlled state politics. They had won most elections, often with the support of the state's Hispanic majority. However, the New Deal changed that. Hispanic New Mexicans liked the New Deal of President Roosevelt, a Democrat.

Thus, Hispanic New Mexicans began to join the Democratic party. They also found a leader they liked. In 1935 Dennis Chávez became United States Senator from New Mexico. Chávez, a Democrat, would serve New Mexicans well until his death in the early 1960s.

CHAPTER FIVE

A Changing Economy Before 1940

Farming and Ranching Become Less Important

When New Mexico became a state, over half its people still made their living from the land. Some did this by farming. Others raised livestock, such as sheep and cattle. Over the years, though, the number of New Mexicans living on the land dropped. Farmers and ranchers faced many hardships. Frequent droughts, such as the Dust Bowl, forced many of them to leave the land. As the number of farms and ranches fell, towns and cities grew. This movement of people to towns and cities is known as urbanization. Fewer people remained in rural areas.

Mining Changes

Mining was also very important when New Mexico became a state. At that time, most miners dug for copper or coal. Copper mining centered at the Santa Rita Mines near Silver City. There mining companies dug large open-pit mines. Using open-cut methods, they cut mining costs and increased production.

Coal mining centered at mines near Raton, Gallup, Madrid, and Carthage. These were "company towns." The owners often provided for the workers' needs. Such an arrangement meant life was often hard and uncertain.

SELECTION FROM
Anarchy and Community in the New American West
Madrid, New Mexico, 1970–2000

The closing of the Madrid mines by Colorado Fuel & Iron (CF&I) in 1906 left one Albuquerque retailer without a source of coal to sell his customers. George Kaseman, one of the founders of Albuquerque's First National Bank, decided to buy the operating leases from CF&I and began operations there the same year, rather than find another supplier. He named his endeavor the Albuquerque and Cerrillos Coal Company, and ran the operations out of Albuquerque from 1906 to 1919. He did little to improve the working or living conditions for the miners. Typical of mining camps, the shacks had no baths, no indoor toilets; few had running water, none had electricity, and all relied on coal stoves for heating and cooking. The boarding houses (probably three) were for single miners, and they had electricity and shower facilities in the basements. The only other buildings with electricity were the company's operations buildings (now part of the museum). The only telephones in town were in the company headquarters, and all incoming and outgoing calls went through the Cerrillos exchange, facilitating company control over the lives of the miners and restricting union organizing.

Before the turn of the century, a few miners built homes in the village (as had been customary before industrialization), but as with most mining camps, under CF&I the bulk of the housing was provided by the company. Kaseman's onsite manager, Oscar Huber, who would become a key figure in Madrid's later history, described why this was so . . . in the early 1900s:

> Miners were more or less of an itinerant group and generally
> without finances. . . . If the mines were to work this was about the
> only class of help available, so somebody had to provide a place
> for them to live and finance them until such time as they produced
> coal. . . . If anyone had suggested at this time that a miner purchase
> his own home the miner would have thought it ridiculous, and the
> company, of course, wanted to maintain the town as a unit which
> they controlled.

There was nothing unusual about this living situation; Madrid was in conformance with the standards of the day. In Madrid, a typical rent for this type of housing in 1916 was two dollars per room per month, including coal for cooking and heating. Fifty cents per month was added on for each electric drop in the house.... Madrid was a middling town, with only the anomaly of its coal types to make it stand out from any other, and its lower rents reflected the lower productive capacities of its coalfields.

Some improvements were made into the second decade of the twentieth century: shacks were wired with a single bulb in each room (again an industry standard); there was a Catholic church (now a private residence); a school for first through fourth grades; a company doctor who treated all the residents, including pregnant women—unusual in coal camps of the day (some of the equipment survives in the museum); a company store with a small post office (the company store is still one of the most substantial buildings in the village and houses a variety of shops, including the original soda fountain); and, to supplement the company store, a mail-order house....

Like all single-enterprise towns, the coal mines at Madrid were the life support for the miners; their fortunes existed in an intricate and unpredictable web of resource availability, national markets, and competition from other sources of energy. What made Madrid slightly different from most western mining operations was the fact that the owner's lifeblood was also so closely tied to those same fortunes. Neither Huber nor Kaseman before him had national or international aspirations; they hoped to maintain at best a regional labor and commodity market edge. In 1928, production peaked at 87,148 tons of anthracite and 97,562 tons of bituminous coal. In that year, 725 miners were employed in the mines. Yet, even during this time of maximum exploitation of the natural resources, the men would listen for the five o'clock whistles to see which mines would be working the next day. Miners at Madrid, as in other mining camps, often hired out as agricultural laborers during slack times. When times were really desperate, as they were during the Depression, they resorted to county welfare. Huber, along with most mine owners, offered scrip in lieu of part of the men's paychecks, and this practice became a powerful tool to keep the men working Huber's mines instead of migrating to more lucrative sites. (Pp. 14–16)

—*Kathryn Hovey*

Demand for coal remained high for many years after World War II. Today, though, copper and coal mining have become less important.

The petroleum (oil) industry grew rapidly in New Mexico after World War I. One oil-producing region was San Juan County. An oil well at the Hogback Field produced oil for the first time in 1922. Shortly afterward drillers struck oil in southeastern New Mexico. In 1922 drillers located natural gas at the Ute Dome Field in San Juan County. But it was in southeastern New Mexico, an area called the Permian Basin, that held the most oil and gas.

SELECTION FROM
Roadside New Mexico
A Guide to Historic Markers

The frontier grasslands of southeastern New Mexico attracted many early twentieth-century homesteaders eager to break the sod and start a new life. One of them, James Hobbs, his wife, Fannie, and their family, which included twin daughters Minnie and Winnie, had originally intended to settle in Alpine, Texas, in hopes that the prairie air would improve Mrs. Hobbs's health. Upon meeting a wagon master coming from that town and hearing his hard-luck story of life there, the Hobbs family decided instead to try the frontier grasslands of southeastern New Mexico. This was ranching land, and when James Berry Hobbs, son of James and Fannie, opened a store and post office around 1909, many of his early customers were area cowboys. The agricultural and ranching settlement that grew near the store took the name of the Hobbs family.

Hobbs might have remained a small but contented trading village had it not been for the discovery of substantial oil reserves beneath the southeastern plains in the early twentieth century. The first commercially successful oil well in New Mexico, the Flynn-Welch-Yates, was drilled between Hobbs and Artesia in 1924. That well tapped the Permian Basin, an almost oval patch of oil reserves underlying a vast region of west Texas and southeastern New Mexico. With proof that the region contained a large body of oil reserves, the "black gold rush" was on.

Hobbs became an oil town on June 13, 1928, when the Midwest State No. 1, sunk by Midwest Oil Company (now Amoco), struck oil at 4,065 feet. This was the "discovery well" for the underlying stretch of oil that soon became known as the "Hobbs field." A sister well, the Bowers No. 1-A, proved equally productive. The result was effectively summarized in the March 15, 1929, edition of the *Lovington Leader* in nearby Lovington:

> Reports coming from the town of Hobbs indicate a rapid and healthy growth of that enterprising little city. A census which was recently taken showed it to have a population of more than 300 and that number has increased since that date. When it is taken into consideration that the town is less than a year old and that most of this growth has taken place within the last two months, it will be readily seen that the record is something to be proud of.

Residents and oil workers erected buildings of more permanence, and a larger Hobbs emerged as population and production proliferated. By April 1930, the month that the Texas–New Mexico Railway arrived in town, Hobbs had, by one estimate, more than ten thousand residents. The city today retains its mix of ranching and oil economies.

The air of the plains, by the way, did improve the health of Fannie Hobbs. She lived in the city she helped form until her death in 1942. Residents lovingly referred to her as "Grandma Hobbs." (Pp. 396–98)

—David Pike

Tourism Becomes More Important

The demand for gasoline rose as more people owned cars. The automobile changed how people lived. They now wanted to travel and see new places. Between 1919 and 1929 western states built more than 1 million miles of highways. They did so with the help of federal funds. In addition, westerners had already fallen in love with their cars. Car ownership by westerners was twice the national average. Californians alone owned 10 percent of the nation's total. And by 1925 more western tourists traveled by car than by train.

In the 1920s Gallup became New Mexico's gateway to the west. Improved roads and cars were putting more and more Americans on wheels. This was especially true in the West. What put Gallup on every tourist's map was Highway 66. It was the country's main east-west highway. From points east it ran all the way across New Mexico. It entered the state east of Tucumcari. It left the state seventeen miles west of Gallup. In between it passed through other New Mexico towns and cities.

But it was Gallup that tourists remembered. Many of them remembered the red sandstone cliffs just east of Gallup. Rising sharply from the ground, these cliffs had long caught the eye of train travelers. Indeed, the railroad had used pictures of the red cliffs in their advertisements.

Most tourists stopped in Gallup for gasoline or a meal. Some spent the night. Those who stayed longer found an enchanting town. Gallup was not an old town in the 1920s. Its history dated back only to the arrival of the railroad in 1881. The town's name derived from the railway paymaster.

Before 1881 sheep and cattle growers lived on the land. Only two buildings stood on the site of the future town. One was a saloon. The other was the Blue Goose General Store built in 1880. It served passengers traveling by the Westward Overland Stage. After 1881 more buildings and new townspeople appeared. In 1891 Gallup became an official town. Further growth gave Gallup its special meaning.

By the 1920s Gallup had become a trade center for the Navajos. Nearby coal mines had attracted miners from as far away as Europe. And in 1922 the town had hosted its first Inter-Tribal Indian Ceremonial. Lighting for the nighttime Indian dances had come from a circle of cars. The 1920s cars had lighted the dances with their carbide headlights.

SELECTION FROM

The Lore of New Mexico

The largest Ceremonial to be seen anywhere in the United States is the Inter-Tribal Indian Ceremonial held annually at Gallup, New Mexico, the last Wednesday, Thursday and Friday in August. The dates this year [1936] are Aug. 26, 27, and 28. At this great tribal conclave more than seven thousand Indians of thirty tribes gather to dance, chant, compete in races, sports and games, and to exhibit their finest arts and crafts. . . .

The Gallup Ceremonial offers more in three days than can be seen at any other time or place in the United States.

During the months preceding the Gallup Ceremonial [Indians] make elaborate preparations. Dancers brighten up their costumes and practice frequently;

athletes train arduously; craftsmen work hard to produce their finest handicrafts. The Ceremonial is a great competition, there being cash prizes for excellence in everything typically Indian.

When all the hundreds of Indian competitors and the thousands of Indians who attend as spectators swarm Gallup for their Ceremonial that little western frontier town becomes more Indian than any town in the country. (P. 374)

—Unidentified newspaper clipping, August 22, 1936

For the tourists passing through, Gallup was the gateway to Arizona and points west. For the tourists who stopped over, Gallup had much to offer.

All through the 1920s and 1930s, visitors came to New Mexico. They came to visit its attractions, such as national and state parks and monuments. Bandelier National Monument was the first. It opened to the public in 1916. Carlsbad Caverns became a National Monument in 1923. In 1930 it became a National Park.

SELECTION FROM

Roadside New Mexico
A Guide to Historic Markers

Jim White, a cowboy building fences near Carlsbad in the late 1890s, first thought the dark, spiraling eddy he saw on the horizon one evening was ash from an erupting volcano. When he investigated, he discovered not smoke but bats, thousands of them, winging en masse from a yawning hole in the side of a mountain. White lit a piece of cactus and tossed it into the abyss to determine the depth of the chasm. The cactus extinguished before reaching the bottom.

White had come across one of the deepest limestone caves in the nation, a cavern penetrating 1,567 dark and damp feet into the earth. Its long history begins in the depths of an ancient sea that covered this area some 240 million years ago. As sea life died, shells, skeletons, and other debris amassed to form what is today known as the Capitan Reef. Over time, the sea evaporated and the reef rose to form the Guadalupe Mountains. Weathering and groundwater fractured the rock within the landform to create these mammoth underground caverns and chambers.

Mescalero Apache Indians in the 1400s were some of the first humans to witness the nightly exodus of bats from the cave. Near the entrance, the Indians cooked within circles of rocks known as ring middens. Whether the Apaches ever entered the cave is not known. However, White certainly did. His partnership with a fertilizer company to mine bat guano for California fruit growers gave the cowboy many opportunities to explore further this subterranean frontier. According to his autobiography, White descended into the cave on a rickety rope-and-stick ladder and dispelled the darkness, which he compared to "a million tons of black wool," with a small kerosene lantern. Water and time had festooned those dark interiors with elegant calcite deposits whose figurative names leave little doubt of their appearance: soda straws, drapery, popcorn, and totem poles. One of the more impressive features White encountered was the 2,013-foot-wide, 254-foot-high "Big Room," today considered the largest subterranean chamber in the United States.

For years, White conducted personal tours of the site and worked to bring recognition to the scenic wonders he found there. In the spring of 1923, he led employees of the General Land Office through an official onsite survey. The scientists were impressed enough to recommend that the site be designated as a national monument. Later that fall, on October 25, President Coolidge officially declared the site as the "Carlsbad Cave National Monument." In 1930, Congress changed the name to Carlsbad Caverns National Park.

After the designation, the National Park Service extended trails, erected staircases, installed electric lighting, and built an elevator to hoist visitors to and from the surface. Tourists converged on the new monument, fascinated by the wonders they found in the Main Corridor, King's Palace, Queen's Chamber, the Big Room, and elsewhere. Several couples even chose to be married near the spectacular formation known as the Rock of Ages, until that practice was ended in 1944.

Jim White, the earliest spelunker of the caves, died in April 1946 at age sixty-four. (Pp. 391–92)

— *David Pike*

Another special New Mexico tourist city was Santa Fe. It dedicated itself after about 1910 to creating a look and feel that set it apart from any other state capital city.

SELECTION FROM
The Lore of New Mexico

La Fonda Hotel on the old Santa Fe Plaza, acquired by the Railroad in 1925 and leased to the Fred Harvey Company in 1926, became the showcase for what became a tricultural blend of architecture, interior decoration, and the merchandising of food, ambience, arts, crafts, and even local residents. One of the first La Fonda brochures proclaimed:

> This old-time city is in the very heart of a region acclaimed by experienced travelers as of continuing and surpassing interest, regardless of the length or season of one's visit. The hospitable doors of La Fonda swing wide the year 'round, for in Old Santa Fe and the surrounding country there is no month of the twelve without its peculiar charm.
>
> From La Fonda radiate tree-bordered avenues and 'dobe-lined byways. Within it comfort and luxury go hand in hand with the true atmosphere of a land where the Past lives on happily with the Present. About it are the things that Kit Carson and Lew Wallace knew—the mountains, the ageless Indian pueblos, the picturesque settlements born in America of a medieval Spain.
>
> Santa Fe's crude fondas of other days were famous as the End of the Trail. La Fonda of today was created to be both the End and Beginning of Trails—for those who would step aside for a time from accustomed things, to follow a hundred new and old ways into the hidden corners of a singularly beautiful and interesting section of our country as yet undisturbed and unspoiled by the rush of modern life.

La Fonda's dining room became the only one in the Fred Harvey system that did not require men to wear a coat and tie, since the Bohemian art colonists would not allow the company to enforce its longstanding rule.

La Fonda was the site of yet another Fred Harvey innovation for transcontinental train travelers: Indian Detours, "an unusual outing-by-motor through the Spanish and Indian Southwest, available [at a cost of forty to sixty dollars per person] as a pleasant break in the long all-rail journey." Major R. Hunter Clarkson, a native of Edinburgh, Scotland, conceived the idea of setting up three-day motor trips between the Castañeda Harvey House in Las Vegas and the Alvarado in Albuquerque, with an intermediate stop at La Fonda. The first Detour brochure, written and designed by Roger W. Birdseye, advised:

> It is the purpose of the Indian Detour to take you through the
> very heart of all this, to make you feel the lure of the Southwest
> that lies beyond the pinched horizons of your train window. In
> no other way can you hope to see so much of a vast, fascinating
> region in so short a time—and with the same economy, the same
> comfort, the same leisurely intimacy and the same freedom from
> all trivial distraction. . . . It is 3 days and 300 miles of sunshine and
> relaxation and mountain air, in a land of unique human contrasts
> and natural grandeur.

The first tourist-carrying Indian Detours Harveycar embarked from Las Vegas on Saturday, May 15, 1926. Couriers, "young women with intimate personal knowledge of the region supplemented by special training," accompanied each Harveycar. Erna Fergusson, who earlier had organized her own guided Koshare Tours to Indian dances, was hired to train the Couriers. They were "expected to be young women of education and some social grace, able to meet easily and well all kinds of people [and] expected to be intelligent enough to learn many facts about this country and to impart them in a way to interest intelligent travelers." An Advisory Board "of nationally known authorities on the archaeology, ethnology and history of the Southwest," including Dr. Edgar Lee Hewett, director of the Museum of New Mexico and the School of American Research, and Charles F. Lummis, selected, instructed, and examined Couriers. (Pp. 83–85)

—Marta Weigle and Peter White

PART TWO

World War II and After

Introduction

On the morning of August 16, 1960, test pilot Joe Kittinger stood at the door of the open balloon gondola. "Highest step in the world," read a sign beneath the door. Looking up, Kittinger saw a black sky. Far below he saw thick clouds. The temperature was well below freezing. The test pilot took a deep breath and jumped into thin air. Down and down he fell toward the New Mexico desert below. After a fall of over four and a half minutes, his main parachute opened. A thankful Kittinger now knew he would land safely. He had proved that man could survive at the edge of space and then return.

This record jump from over 18 miles above the earth was the last for Operation Manhigh. This project tested how humans functioned near the edge of space. Manhigh had its headquarters at Holloman Air Force Base. The desert near Alamogordo had proved a good place for space research. Manhigh and projects like it showed how New Mexico had changed during and after World War II.

In Part II you will read about New Mexico's role in World War II. You will learn how New Mexico's economy has developed in recent years. In addition, you will learn what changes have occurred in Indian and Hispanic ways of living.

CHAPTER SIX

World War II

World War II Begins

On December 7, 1941, Americans went to war again. On that day Japan attacked the United States. They bombed the naval base at Pearl Harbor in Hawai'i. They sank or damaged several United States warships. They then attacked other American bases in the Pacific. A major target was the Philippines.

Just hours into the war, New Mexicans came under fire. Some 1,800 of them helped defend the Philippines. They belonged to the 200th Coastal Artillery Regiment. The army told them to protect Clark Field, America's largest airbase in the Pacific. When Japanese airplanes hit the airfield, the New Mexicans fired back. They managed to shoot down some enemy fighters. From the first day, then, New Mexicans were in the thick of the fighting.

The next day, 500 men of the 200th formed a new unit, the 515th. Together, these two units withdrew with other American troops to the Bataan Peninsula. There they fought bravely. The hungry and outnumbered men on Bataan finally surrendered on April 9, 1942. After the war, the commander at Bataan said this of the New Mexicans: "First to fire, and last to lay down their arms. . . ."

New Mexicans Are War Heroes

What followed was the Bataan Death March. The Japanese marched the captives 65 miles in the hot sun to a railroad. The prisoners had little food or water. They marched for six days and 11,000 prisoners died.

Trains then took some surviving captives to a Japanese prison camp.
Ships took still others to prison camps in Japan. On board these ships
yet more captives died. Within the camps, thousands more died. Many
were New Mexicans. Of the 1,800 New Mexicans who served on Bataan,
only 900 returned home. A Bataan Memorial was built at Fort Bliss,
Texas. Later moved to Santa Fe, the memorial includes our state's eter-
nal flame. It honors the brave New Mexicans who fought and died in
the Philippines.

Also honoring all New Mexico's military wounded is the Purple Heart
Trail, which follows Interstate 40 across the state.

New Mexicans Help the War Effort

World War II lasted nearly four years. During that time over 50,000 New
Mexicans served in the armed forces. They saw action against not only
Japan, but also Germany and Italy. One group from New Mexico and
Arizona played a special role in fighting Japan. These were the Navajo
Code Talkers. The Marine Corps needed a way to send messages quickly
by radio. They used Navajo marines to do this. The Japanese did not
understand Navajo. Little of it had been written down. The Code Talkers
developed a secret code of their own. For instance, they referred to dive
bombers as "Chicken Hawks." Anti-tank guns were "Tortoise Killers."
Even untrained Navajos who listened to the code did not know what it
meant. One Marine recruit who became a Code Talker was Carl Gorman.

SELECTION FROM
Carl Gorman's World

These were the early tragic days after Pearl Harbor, Corregidor, and the series
of naval disasters. Not only did the Japanese have superior arms, position, and
equipment, they were breaking our tightest communication codes, and the
result was death and destruction to the American armed forces.

By the time Carl Gorman had reached the Marine recruiting station at
Fort Defiance, a plan had already been developed that would involve him personally in one of the most important secret operations in American military
history. It was to be the creation of a military code for combat and invasion

purposes that the enemy would never break. And the men destined for this assignment were to be Navajos.

It was a non-Indian, strangely enough, who was presenting the idea responsible for this invulnerable code. He was Philip Johnston, an American engineer who had grown up on the reservation, a missionary's son, who learned to speak Navajo fluently as a child. He had the brilliant, simple concept of using the Navajo language as the basis for a new military code. He knew that it was unbelievably difficult and virtually unknown anywhere else in the world. Johnston excitedly proposed his idea before the Marine top brass at Camp Elliott in California. At first they thought he was insane. He refused to give up. He brought in several Navajos from Los Angeles whom he briefed on how to present a rough code from Navajo to English, and he dramatically proved his case. No cryptography, no code machines. Only a Navajo sender at one end and a Navajo receiver at the other, who translated the message into English, and it worked!

The Japanese were already on Guadalcanal in the summer of 1942, breaking all the American codes. From Marine headquarters, a guarded authorization went out for a pilot test group of thirty Navajos to develop the new code. Time was crucial. Recruits had to be found at once who spoke Navajo and English well. They came from the reservation boarding schools and from faraway hogans, too. Most had never gone more than a few score miles from their native homes, and some were so young they forged their age to enlist. All were inducted at Fort Wingate, and Carl Gorman was one of these volunteers. They had no knowledge as yet of the true nature of their mission. All they were told was that they were in special service. There were twenty-nine as they were taken by train through the night to Camp Elliott in California (one of the selected thirty just never showed up). Some were light-hearted. Most were filled with fear, with a sense of being swept into the unknown. They had been jolted quickly into a harsh, unfamiliar world, from the land and homes in which they had spent their young lives. Carl Gorman understood their silence, their withdrawn behavior. He was twice the age of many of them. . . .

At Camp Elliott these Navajo recruits were assigned to one platoon. They quickly adjusted to what the Americans called "tough training." They had been toughened by the land where they lived, had known extreme heat and cold, extreme hunger and thirst. What was so rough about a basic training hike with an eighty-pound pack on their back, when they thought nothing of walking twenty miles from their hogans to a distant trading post and return-ing home again with a pack of provisions on their shoulders? They regarded the harshness of training with Navajo humor. "This Marine stuff is noth-ing," one of them said, laughing, "compared to the hell we had to take in the boarding schools." There was a good deal of prejudice at first. Some of the Marines started off by calling them "Chief" in derision. After the Navajos proved they could take the training, the word became more and more an easy greeting. They had their worst problem with their drill sergeant, a lanky Tennessean with a shrill voice and a manner to match. He was determined to make Marines out of these "lousy Indians." When they kept their hands in their pockets, even for a moment, he filled their pockets with sand and made them drill that way. He cursed them when they changed his "hup-two-three-four" to their own cadence in Navajo. He resented their growing esprit de corps, resented Carl Gorman's growing strength as one of the leaders of the platoon. He did more than push their training. He appeared determined to take out his own personal venom on their darker alien skins. Unexpectedly, he met his match in Carl Gorman.

The Navajo platoon was lined up one morning waiting for their drill sergeant. The moment he arrived he said abruptly, "I'm going to give you clowns a boxing lesson." Moving slowly, officiously down the line of men, he plowed his fist into one Navajo face after the other. The young boys reeled back, some falling from the blow. The tenth man in line was Carl Gorman, who watched the scene with mounting anger. He remembered everything he had learned as an expert boxer in his youth at Albuquerque. He was prepared when his turn came. He skillfully ducked the sergeant's fist. He swiftly hit him with a one-two punch, knocking him flat. The Navajos roared with laughter.

Carl was the hero of the moment. Word of the incident spread rapidly about the camp, even to the CO's office. This act of a raw recruit—an Indian—smashing his fist into the face and the authority of a Marine drill sergeant was unprecedented. The immediate result of such an act could have been a court martial and a year in the brig at hard labor, but nothing was done. The drill sergeant made no report. The officers chose to overlook the incident. In view of the circumstance, it was deemed wisest for all concerned to let the matter lie.

There was, in fact, very little prejudice as the Navajos' training went on.

There were pep talks, stimulating the boys to think positively beyond their present situation and toward the time when the war would be over. One drill instructor, Sergeant Stephenson, made a strong impression on Carl Gorman. He lectured the men about the importance of having a goal in life and talked to them about determination. "Never say you can't do something," he reiterated. "If someone tells you to move the Statue of Liberty to the West Coast, you don't say how—you say when?"

The excitement and the hard work of drawing up the Navajo code began. The Navajos were to create the code themselves. It was a group effort, all of the men in the original twenty-nine participating with Carl. It was to be a military code that would never be written down, except for training purposes, and then the papers would be destroyed. The training books were locked up every night. The code would be carried over radio or by wire from one talking transmitter to another, and then instantly decoded. The difficult task for the Navajos was to prepare hundreds of key words and military phrases that could be memorized and used efficiently, for urgent communication. Words had to be easily, instantaneously recognized under harsh battle conditions. And there must never be the slightest chance of a mistake.

A whole assortment of military words had to be invented to be used in Navajo. They began with the word for "corps." It became a Navajo word for one of their clans. There was great laughing and yelling as the boys argued for their own family clan name. A division became "salt"; a regiment, "edgewater"; a squad, "black sheep."

It became an exciting game, as they went on to search for the appropriate word. Airplanes became "birds." A bomber was a "buzzard"; a fighter plane, a "hummingbird"; a patrol plane a "crow." Ships became "fish." A battleship was a "whale"; a minesweeper, a "beaver"; a destroyer, "a shark." A route became a "rabbit trail"; a convoy was "moving on water"; a bomb was an "egg."

The alphabet was based on easily remembered words beginning with English letters familiar in the Navajo culture. *A* was for "ant" ("woll-a-chee"). *J* was for "jackass" (tkele-cho-gi), *S* for sheep ("dibeh"), *Y* for "yucca" ("tsah-as-zih").

This was a fantastic requirement that was demanded of the Navajo boys: to memorize so much in the urgent timetable of only a few weeks, the hundreds of words and phrases, most of them foreign to their own basic culture. But it was a feat Carl Gorman knew would not be insurmountable. He tried to explain why to the communication officer, who was amazed at the speed with which the Navajo boys were drilling. "You have to understand," Carl Gorman said, "that for us, everything is memory. You see, Lieutenant, it's part of our heritage. We have no written language. Our songs, our prayers, our stories, they're all handed down from grandfather to father to children—and we listen, we hear, we learn to remember everything. It's part of our training."

The Navajos, caught up in the excitement of building their code, began testing each other, message after message, in terse Marine Corps instructions: "Machine gun fire on left flank. . . ," "Platoon 4 to dig in. Losses running high. . . . " "Change coordinates, numbers as follows. . . . " In a testing demonstration before the military staff, they astounded the officers with the speed of their communications. With two Navajos separated at a considerable distance, Carl Gorman behind one barracks wall and his friend, Bill McCabe, behind another, a six-line coded message was completed in exactly two minutes; it was sent to a receiver in Navajo and delivered back in English!

"It goes in, in Navajo? And it comes out in English?" an officer exclaimed. "How does that work?" he thundered at Carl Gorman.

"It's very simple, sir," Carl said to him. "It's because that's the talking code machine over there where my Navajo friend McCabe is and I'm a talking code machine over here."

From that day on, the term *Code Talkers* stayed with the Navajos. Three of the navy's best-trained intelligence experts were brought in to test their messages, intercepting them, attempting to break them down. They failed completely, detecting no basic pattern. The new code seemed foolproof. It was ready for testing under combat conditions. (Pp. 57–60)

—*Henry Greenberg and Georgia Greenberg*

The Japanese never broke the code. Many marines owed their lives to the speedy messages sent in Navajo. The Code Talkers were so successful that the Marine Corps kept their work secret for over twenty years. In 2001 the United States finally honored the Code Talkers. The twenty-nine Navajos who developed the code were awarded the Congressional Gold Medal. About 400 Indian soldiers were part of the Code Talkers, including Chotaw, Sioux, Comanche, Kiowa, Hopi, and Cherokee. These Indians, too, received Congressional Medals in 2001.

The Science of Warfare

At home, the open lands of New Mexico made it a center of military activity. Air bases for training pilots sprang up around the state. The government built large prisoner of war camps here. The state had for a while been a center for rocket research. During the war, Los Alamos, New Mexico, became the center for top secret atomic research.

But Los Alamos was not alone among New Mexico communities in matching science to warfare. It was not the first, either—Roswell was.

SELECTION FROM
New Mexico's History
A Message for the Future

There is a story that when the Second World War ended the United States government began an inquiry about Germany's V-2 rockets that terrorized London. When questioned, one German scientist reputedly replied that the United States needed to pay more attention to Robert Goddard.

Dr. Robert Hutchings Goddard was born in Worcester, Massachusetts, in 1882. He attended Worcester Polytechnic where he taught physics while working on his masters and doctorate degrees from Clark University. He initially worked as a research fellow at Princeton University in 1912 and then, in 1914, accepted a job at his alma mater, where he would be a professor of physics for the next twenty-nine years.

Goddard had a genius, an intellectual strength that he combined with a shy gentleness and firm sense of mission. Many people saw him as a personification of the mad genius but others like Charles Lindbergh, Harry F. Guggenheim, and his college President, Wallace Atwood, recognized him as a visionary genius. They were correct, for he became a pioneering scientist.

As early as seventeen years old and before the turn-of-the-century, Goddard spoke and wrote about upper atmosphere space travel. He would pursue that idea for the rest of his life, becoming, as some have described, the man who made the greatest contribution to the development of rockets and space travel.

His early research work concentrated on rocketry even before the first airplane! In 1908 he conducted static tests of solid-fuel rockets. Then he developed the idea of using liquid hydrogen and oxygen for multi-stage interplanetary rockets. When he joined the faculty at Clark University, he began experimenting with larger rockets. Here he began investigations into liquid propellant rockets but was interrupted by the First World War.

During the war he worked on and developed several types of solid propellant rockets for defense against the newly developed tanks then being used. As a result, he perfected the Bazooka that became an integral weapon in the Second World War.

After the war, Goddard continued his rocket work. In 1926 at Auburn, Massachusetts, he conducted a career-changing test when he launched his first successful liquid-fuel rocket flight. This was the first rocket flight to carry on board instruments. The rocket carried a barometer, thermometer and a camera to photograph the other two instruments. The eleven-foot, six-inch rocket rose vertically to ninety feet and then traveled a horizontal distance of one hundred feet. Fortunately, no one was hurt. Nor was anyone's property damaged. But the potential for such accidents plus the subsequent publicity of that test convinced Goddard, if not the local authorities, that he needed to relocate to a place where he could conduct his tests safely.

Thus, with the funding of the Daniel and Florence Guggenheim Foundation, he moved to Roswell, New Mexico. There, in the open spaces of eastern New Mexico, Dr. Goddard worked in a small laboratory outside of town where his production was astounding. For the next decade and a half, Dr. Goddard worked and produced. He fired a rocket that traveled faster than the speed of sound. He developed push-button launches that started a process of devices that operated before the launch. He is credited with devising deflector vanes to stabilize and guide the rocket. He was the first person to demonstrate that rockets will function in a vacuum. Among his many other ideas such as self-cooling rocket motors and landing devices, he forecast jet-driven airplanes and travel in space.

When the Second World War broke out Dr. Goddard moved to Annapolis to work for the Navy. He worked on a number of special projects, probably the most important of which was his work on jet-assisted takeoff devices for aircraft. He died in Annapolis on 10 August 1945 before he completed his work. But Dr. Goddard would never have finished his work.

Since his death, this mild scientist has received many honors. Scholarships and awards, as well as buildings and libraries are named for him. His laboratory, tools, and several pieces of his equipment are permanently preserved in the Robert H. Goddard Planetarium of the Roswell Museum and Art Center in Roswell. There the visitor can view a permanent exhibition about him.

He was a man whose genius continues to benefit all mankind. No longer considered weird for his ideas, he became a significant part of New Mexico's scientific legacy. (Forthcoming)

— *Thomas E. Chávez*

The Atomic Age Begins

Work on the atomic bomb occurred at Los Alamos. These efforts were the single most significant use of science for warfare. The bomb and the idea behind it were new. Not even those who built the bomb knew if it would work. First it had to be tested. This test took place at Trinity Site on the White Sands Proving Ground near Alamogordo. The date was July 16, 1945.

The test was a success. In fact, the blast was heard or the flash was seen all over the state. One traveler had just crossed from New Mexico into Arizona when "Suddenly, the tops of high mountains by which we were passing were lighted up by a reddish, orange light. . . . Then it was dark again. . . . It was just like the sun had come up and suddenly gone down again."

Still, the new bomb remained a secret for three more weeks. Only after an atomic bomb was dropped on Japan did people everywhere learn of the new weapon. The site was Hiroshima, Japan. The date was August 6, 1945. In an instant 75,000 Japanese died.

President Harry S. Truman had made the decision to use the bomb. He thought its use would save hundreds of thousands of American lives. He believed its use would force the Japanese to surrender. Japan did surrender to the United States. However, Japan surrendered only after a second atomic bomb was used. The United States dropped this bomb on Nagasaki, Japan, on August 9.

With the surrender of Japan, World War II ended. New Mexico and its people had played a major role in the war effort. New Mexico was, among other things, the birthplace of the atomic age. It has remained a center of atomic research ever since. Today, Los Alamos National Laboratory carries on research for the Department of Energy. But Los Alamos's story could not be told until after the war ended. Los Alamos was a "secret city" during and immediately after World War II. Slowly, though, people were told about what had been done there. Los Alamos's research had changed the world.

SELECTION FROM
The Day the Sun Rose Twice
The Story of the Trinity Site Nuclear Explosion July 16, 1945

The secret atomic city in the mountains of northern New Mexico contained the *crème de la crème* of the Manhattan Project.

The Los Alamos site was created for two main reasons. First, the project needed a special weapons laboratory that would put the bomb together. Second, and probably more important, General Groves (in charge of the Manhattan Project) faced massive security regulations. From the beginning, he had insisted that the people involved with the various aspects of the Manhattan Project know only enough to carry out their own jobs effectively. This "compartmentalization" of tasks lay at the heart of all Manhattan Project security. It proved so effective that no information ever reached German hands. . . .

In early 1942, Groves decided that the project needed to create a new, isolated site where the scientists could all come together and talk openly. So, in the summer of 1942, after a brief search, Groves, Major John Dudley, and the newly appointed head of this installation, California physicist J. Robert Oppenheimer, selected the region of Los Alamos, New Mexico. Oppenheimer had known and loved this area for years, for his family had had a ranch in the nearby Pecos Mountains. Here he was able to combine his two great loves—physics and New Mexico. Moving swiftly, the government took over the facilities of an exclusive boys' preparatory school and the lands of about twenty-six other area inhabitants. Much was already government owned and soon a total of about 9,000 acres was acquired for the war effort. Oppenheimer assumed that facilities would be needed to house perhaps thirty scientists and their families. The "realists" of the time argued that they would need room for at least 500. At the end of the war, close to 6,500 people were living on the Hill.

In early 1943, Mrs. Dorothy McKibbin, a widow in her mid-forties, was hired to run the front office at 109 East Palace Avenue in Santa Fe. Everything that went to the Hill passed through her doors. One of the unsung heroines of the Manhattan Project, Dorothy McKibbin directed lost scientists and nervous soldiers to the proper buses, while politely but firmly discouraging those who did not belong. When uninvited people arrived seeking work, she played dumb and sent them away. About twelve couples were married at her adobe home on the Old Santa Fe Trail, and her gracious charm smoothed many a ruffled feather. "It's been the most exciting job in the world," she confessed later.

From 1943 to 1945, the tiny community of Los Alamos, New Mexico, formed an unreal world, part mountain resort and part military base. Locally it was often termed "the Magic Mountain" or "Shangri-La. . . . "

The reasons for this atmosphere were many. To begin with, the physical environment could hardly be surpassed. At 7,400 feet, Los Alamos (the name means "the poplars") is surrounded by the towering peaks of the Sangre de Cristo mountain range, some reaching 13,000 feet. Abrupt mesas, the world's largest extinct volcano crater (the Valle Grande), numerous ancient Indian ruins, bustling modern Indian Pueblos, and tiny Spanish-American villages still speaking a seventeenth-century patois all lie within an hour's drive. The summers are cool and dry, and the winters offer both skiing and skating. Spring and fall provide ideal opportunities for hikes or horseback rides through the surrounding countryside. The area still is one of the most striking in the continental United States.

More important than the scenery, however, was the deep sense of purpose that the group shared. The men and women at Los Alamos formed an international community that was engaged in a life-or-death struggle to beat the Germans to the secret of atomic power. This goal gave the town its fierce intensity. In 1975, physicist Hans A. Bethe confessed that never, either before or after, had he worked as hard as he did during his years at Los Alamos. "It was one of the few times in my life," said another well-known physicist, "when I felt truly alive."

Oppenheimer recruited many of the top personnel himself. His job was made easier by the fact that the scientists knew they would be applying their talents for the benefit of their country. They also knew that if they succeeded, they would become a part of history. . . . After some initial hesitation, recruitment snowballed, and by 1944 virtually every American physicist of importance was involved in the project. . . .

Even those at Los Alamos who knew little about the activities behind the fenced-in "Tech Area," knew that they were producing something "that would help end the war." When the scientists returned from the Trinity explosion, a custodian rushed up to physicist Fred Reines, grabbed his hand, and said, "Well, we did it, didn't we?" "Yes," said Reines, "we sure did." This commitment pervaded all levels of society.

One must add that the men and women of Los Alamos were then young. The average age was around twenty-seven. . . . Many couples began their families while living on the mesa. Nearly one thousand babies were born in that small community from 1943 to 1949; those 208 born during the war had birth certificates listing the place as simply Box 1663, Sandoval County, Rural.

It is probably safe to say that never before in the history of the human race have so many brilliant minds been gathered together at one place. . . .

When one considers how many people worked at Los Alamos itself, let alone the Manhattan Project in general, the army's success in concealing its purpose was phenomenal. It became, indeed, "the best kept secret of the war." (Pp. 15–23)

—Ferenc Szasz

CHAPTER SEVEN

New Mexico's Indian Peoples

Indians from New Mexico served with distinction in all branches of the military in World War II. Whether in the Pacific or in Europe, they fought to defeat fascism and defend democracy. Their wartime experiences differed little from those of other soldiers. But their heritage and traditions shaped how they viewed the war and themselves. Many Indian soldiers were forever changed by the war. They now wanted to live in "two worlds." They were Indians who found ways to be true to their heritage in society at large. Living in "two worlds" began in World War II. It continued when Indian soldiers returned home.

SELECTION FROM

A Zuni Life

A Pueblo Indian in Two Worlds

The formal signing of Germany's surrender took place on May 8, 1945, and suddenly we had nothing to do but wait for the Army to decide where we would go next. . . .

All we could think about then was going home. Whatever came after would come. Our mail caught up with us, but it didn't make anything easier for most of the guys. Those who got good news could hardly wait to get back, and those who got bad news wondered why they had fought so hard. I had good news. My brother, Lee, had joined the Navy and was in the Pacific, but was still all right. . . .

My mother and sisters and aunts had sent me cookies, all crushed, but I guess they'd been thinking about me. I also got another packet of corn meal.

I'd been running low, using just little pinches to offer the gods. The corn meal had worked. I'd gone through some of the fiercest fighting of the war and never had a scratch, or even a cold. It was my own secret weapon.

I also had some bad news. The girl I'd left back home had found another guy, like I thought she might. Part of it was my fault. I'd promised to write every day, but that hadn't been possible over the past months in Europe. . . .

We knew we were home when we saw the Statue of Liberty in New York Harbor waiting for us. Everyone was shouting and waving, much different than when we'd left. We'd been pretty quiet then. They had us off the ship, into trucks, and back in Camp Shanks by noon. I'd never seen the army move so fast. The camp commanders greeted us and told us to throw our old "C" rations away, because we'd be eating steak for supper, and they kept their promise. That was a first, too.

Within a week, they'd processed us all, sending us to the army posts nearest our homes. I was on a train for three days before I got back to Fort Bliss, Texas, the first week in August. Almost the first thing they did was to give us our back pay. I'd drawn partial pay of ten dollars only twice in all the time I'd been gone, and that's all the money I'd seen. I hadn't needed it. I was surprised when they figured up how much they owed me. First, base pay for a private was fifty dollars a month. I'd been promoted twice: to private first class and corporal, and each promotion came with a pay raise. I'd been given the Infantry Combat Badge, which was worth another ten dollars a month. Overseas pay and combat pay both added bonus money. I had hundreds of dollars in my hand when I left the pay tent. They said there'd be more when I came back from furlough. To celebrate, I got a pass to El Paso, the town nearest the post, and found a good Mexican cafe where I could get a bowl of chile and some enchiladas. I made a hog of myself, but it was sure good.

It took three or four days to process the paperwork for my thirty-day furlough to Zuni. That was the army I was used to. Before I left the post, the papers were filled with news about the dropping of the atomic bomb on Hiroshima. They were predicting the end of the war. That was all right with me, but I didn't believe it.

I called Zuni and left word for my uncle and my sisters that I'd be taking the bus to Gallup and when it would arrive, as there was no public transportation from Gallup to Zuni. When I arrived in Gallup, my uncle was waiting for me in his pickup truck. He had a medicine man with him, a man I knew. Before we crossed the Zuni River, my uncle stopped the truck and the medicine man blessed me with corn meal, brushing me down with an eagle wing fan, taking away all the evil I might have brought with me from where I'd been. They didn't want me to bring disease back to the pueblo. They wrapped up whatever they found in corn husk and had me throw it into the river. I think maybe the medicine men can see whatever it is they clean you of, but I don't know.

My mother cried when I came into the house, she was so glad I was home. She'd fixed everything I liked to eat. People came to see me, and I visited everyone wearing my uniform with my corporal stripes. It was just like on my last furlough, except this time everyone wanted to know about the fighting. I didn't want to talk about it, so I just gave general answers, which worked just as well. Even my old girlfriend, the one who sent me the "Dear John" letter, talked to me and asked me to come back to her. I said no. Even though we heard the war was over with Japan, I knew I'd have to go back in the army. . . .

I was three days late getting back to Fort Bliss, but they just yelled at me. I knew they wouldn't do anything to me. They shipped me to Camp Bulkner in North Carolina for jungle training. The army thought we'd still have to defeat the Japanese on each of the Pacific Islands they held. . . .

Our colonel didn't work us very hard because he knew it was all a waste of time. I used to go on leave to Greensboro every weekend and eat steak. I got paid every month now. We sat around until February before I received orders to go back to Fort Bliss for discharge. There I sat around some more, doing very little, until April, when I actually was separated from the army.

I asked my uncle to pick me up at Gallup again and went back to being an Indian. I hauled wood, herded sheep, and helped with the crops. I even helped take care of my uncle's hogs, as I'd learned at the Albuquerque Indian School. We cut and baled alfalfa for the horses, heavy dirty work. Little bits of hay got under my shirt and itched, just like the old days. . . .

I was just drifting and I wanted to do something with my life, so I decided to go to the University of New Mexico on the G.I. Bill and study to become an electrical engineer. I had visions of bringing electricity to Zuni. . . .

A lot of anthropologists at the University were good to me because I was an Indian. I used to babysit for Dr. John Adair's children and always looked forward to going there because he fed me. . . . I also worked for Dr. Florence Hawley, the anthropologist, helping with anything she could find for me to do to make a little spending money.

I was pretty active socially at the time, and that was expensive. I borrowed money sometimes from a close Anglo friend, telling him I'd pay him when my grandfather sold the wool. By this time, we were roommates, living in Albuquerque's Martíneztown barrio. I didn't tell him they wouldn't sell the wool until spring, so I had quite a debt to pay when my money finally came. I think he was beginning to wonder if he'd ever get paid back, but he didn't say anything.

I took college math and bookkeeping and English. . . . I learned more outside of class than in class, though the bookkeeping course came in handy later. Engineering students told me I was in the wrong field if I wanted to be an electrician. Engineers work in factories, not out in rural areas designing electrical systems for housing. They told me what I really wanted was to become an electrical contractor. They said there was only one way to become one: work for some years as a state-licensed electrician's helper and then take a licensing test. In order to qualify to take the test, you had to have the licensed electrician sign an affidavit swearing you'd put in your time. They also said that the trade skills—carpentry, masonry, and others, as well as electrical contracting—were controlled by Whites and Mexicans. A licensed, skilled craftsman was most likely to take his own son, or nephew, as a helper. That's still true. Back then, there weren't any Zuni electrical contractors I could apprentice to, and neither the Mexicans nor the Whites wanted to let Indians into the trade.

At that time, even though I'd risked my life fighting overseas, I could neither vote nor drink alcohol in New Mexico under state law because I was an Indian. When we'd go once a week for supper at the Pig Stand Cafe, across from the University, I'd ask for a beer and a soup and sandwich to tease the waitress and make the others laugh. I didn't really want the beer because I still didn't like the taste of it. But if the state of New Mexico wouldn't even let me buy a beer, I figured I didn't have much chance of making them give me an opportunity to become an electrician.

I dropped out of school and got a job in a factory in Albuquerque, making venetian blinds. After a few months there, I applied to Maisel's Indian Trading Post and got a job making silver and turquoise jewelry. At Maisel's, I became friends with a Santo Domingo Indian. He'd heard about a job in Los Alamos, planting shrubs and flowers for Baker Brothers Nursery that paid better. It was outside work, so we went to work there. That ended when winter came. I went back to Zuni, no farther along in my search for a career than when I started.

The following spring the superintendent of the Bureau of Indian Affairs told me about a job as maintenance man for the Civil Aeronautics Administration office in Black Rock. I applied and got the job, working there for three years to save up enough money to buy a three-quarter ton pickup truck. We needed the truck to haul wood and farm supplies. On the job, I learned something about the maintenance of motors and generators, which was interesting to me because they ran with electricity. I felt I was getting closer to what I wanted to do.

My other responsibility at the CAA was to climb to the top of Dowa Yallane, where there was a beacon, and change the light bulb on the tower when it burned out. It took me almost a day to climb the mountain and come back. My boss used to say: "Take the rest of the day off. It was more than a day's work." He was a good boss.

Things were looking up. The tribe appointed me bookkeeper, which was easy for me because I'd taken bookkeeping at UNM. There wasn't much in the way of revenue back then. From time to time, I'd give a financial report at a council meeting. It was my first taste of politics and I liked it. The veterans organized a local American Legion Post and I was elected vice-commander. Pretty good for a corporal. The girls still thought I was good-looking, so even that was all right.

I got laid off in May of 1951 and started looking for a job again. In the meantime, there was still plenty of work in the field helping my father haul alfalfa, watermelons, and cantaloupes to Gallup to sell. The melons went for fifteen to twenty cents apiece. It was good money then. The rest we gave away to relatives, so they wouldn't go to waste.

The waiting started bothering me. I didn't want to just work for my father the rest of my life. By 1953, I was sick. I had developed stomach trouble and was nervous and short-tempered. I had nightmares about combat. My mother and father were worried about me. They said my condition came from seeing all those dead bodies and being shot at. John Adair, the anthropologist I used to babysit for when I went to school at UNM, was working in Zuni and he noticed it, too. A friend of his from Cornell University came visiting him, and he said if it were not taken care of I could go crazy and eventually die of it. They call it post-combat syndrome now.

My parents asked my grandfather to help me. He belonged to the Newekwe clown society, and they knew how to cure problems like mine. He started me on a four-day cure that began each morning when he'd come to

the house and mix herbs for me to drink. I'd vomit four times before noon.
At the end of the fourth day, he told me I'd get over it. He was right. My
parents noticed that over the next two months I showed signs of improving.
I no longer had nightmares and had started treating them with respect, not
showing temper like I had before.

When you get cured by the Newekwe, you have to join the society. There
are two levels, the clowns who attend the masked dances, with whom everyone is familiar, and the officers, who know how to cure. I became a clown.
The clowns represent the people, just as the masked dancers represent the
gods. Since the first times, the people keep forgetting the instructions the gods
gave them about how to live and the clowns act out the mistakes, getting everything backward. Sometimes, they also make fun of people who cause scandal
in the pueblo. They talk pretty dirty, but the people laugh. I performed whenever I was asked.

I was thirty years old in 1954 and had about given up any thought of doing
anything in the world. It looked like I'd be a traditional Zuni Indian, like my
father and grandfather. There was nothing wrong with that. It just wasn't what
I'd planned for my life.

The Bureau of Indian Affairs brought electricity to the pueblo and I didn't
have anything to do with it. I didn't like what happened because of it. When
masked dances were held, the young people would stay inside the houses lis-
tening to rock and roll music on their radios instead of watching. I don't like
rock music even now. . . .

I kept looking for work away from the pueblo, dissatisfied with what was
happening to Zuni and to me. Finally, I heard there were job openings at the
Fort Wingate Army Depot, just east of Gallup. After a job interview and some
waiting, I got a letter to report for work on August 11, 1954. I was on my way.
(Pp. 39–50)

—Virgil Wyaco

World War II altered people's lives. It brought some lasting changes
for Indian society, too. During the war some Indian families left their
homes. They found jobs elsewhere. Some worked in wartime industries.
Others worked in agriculture. After the war more and more Indians began
attending school. This trend continues; schools in Indian communities are
important sources of change.

SELECTION FROM
Native Peoples of the Southwest

When Navajo veterans returned from World War II, they were alarmed by the lack of educational facilities for their children. Once considered to be an intrusive element that attacked the foundations of Navajo culture, educational institutions were regarded by the returning servicemen as necessary to the survival of the Navajo people. Previously children had gone without school-ing because their roles as sheepherders took priority over American-style schooling, but after World War II the Navajo demanded more local schools to replace the boarding schools and the few scattered BIA schools on the reser-vation. In the 1950s, when the bureau, the states, and the tribe collaborated to fund schools for Navajo children, thousands of Navajo children were able, for the first time, to attend school and return to their families at night.

Between 1950 and 1960 enrollment more than doubled, and the tribal council established a $10 million scholarship fund to finance the college and university education of an increasing number of young Navajos. Today Navajos send their children to mission schools, BIA boarding and day schools, public schools, or community-controlled contract schools. Locally elected school boards hire employees to run contract schools, so named because contracts with the BIA supply at least partial funding. The existence of day schools means that only children in the most remote areas must attend boarding schools; the Navajo Nation's Head Start program offers early childhood education.

The Navajo Nation was among the first Indian tribes to develop innova-tive programs that integrated Navajo culture with Anglo-American education and job-skills training, such as those at Rough Rock and Rock Point Demon-stration Schools in 1966. In 1968 the Navajos opened Navajo Community College (now known as Diné College), the first locally controlled Indian col-lege of its kind. Post-secondary education is available at Navajo Community College, with main campuses in Tsaile, Arizona, and Shiprock, New Mexico; Crownpoint Institute of Technology in New Mexico offers vocational and technical training. The college, guided by the Diné philosophy of learning, has a curriculum based on Navajo principles of honoring and maintaining bal-ance in the universe. Navajo culture, including history, language, and medi-cal knowledge and practice, is formally taught. Funding is federal, tribal, and private. Wilson Aronilth Jr., a professor in the Navajo studies program at Diné College, explained the importance of Navajo education: "The heart of Diné education lies within ourselves, in our language, in our native culture, in our own values, in our own beliefs, in our history, in our arts and crafts, in nature and in the Holy People. When we understand our own education, then we will have self understanding: where we came from, whom we came from, who we are, what we are, why we are here and where we are going. We will then walk in beauty and everything will finish in beauty."

In spite of such innovative programs, in 1990 only 41.2 percent of the Navajo Nation, in comparison to 75.2 percent of the general U.S. population, had graduated from high school, while only 2.9 percent of Navajos on the reservation, versus 20.3 percent of the general population, had earned bachelor's degrees.

Today, the challenge is not to enroll Navajo students in school but to encourage them to graduate. In 1990 there were 37,808 Navajos under ten years old on the reservation, making them by far the largest percentage of the population. (Pp. 342–44)

—Trudy Griffin-Pierce

Miguel Trujillo Gains the Right to Vote

Indians also saw their political power grow after World War II. In early 1948 New Mexico's reservation Indians still could not vote. An Isleta Pueblo man, Miguel Trujillo, changed this. Trujillo had served in the Marines in World War II. He had graduated from the University of New Mexico and was a schoolteacher. Now in 1948 he wanted to vote. But the county clerk would not let him register.

The county clerk said New Mexico law would not allow him to vote. New Mexico law said Indians on reservations were "untaxed." They did not have to pay property taxes on reservation land. Thus, the law said, Indians could not vote. Trujillo thought the law unfair and decided to challenge it. Strangely, some Indians opposed Trujillo. They believed gaining the vote would hurt them. They feared gaining the vote might allow the government to take away some of their rights. They were most worried about the right to rule themselves.

Trujillo took his case to court anyway. In August 1948 the court ruled in his favor. Miguel Trujillo could vote. So could all other reservation

Indians. The court said that Indians paid all other taxes except the property tax. To deny them the right to vote was unfair. Today few people
remember Miguel Trujillo. But his contribution to progress in New Mexico
was great. Being able to vote brought another right. Now all Indians could
also run for public office in New Mexico.

United States Indian Policy Changes
Throughout the Twentieth Century

After World War II and especially in the 1950s the United States changed
its policy toward Indians. Tribes had been encouraged to be self-sufficient
for about twenty years. But Congress adopted new laws known as "termination legislation." Under this plan American Indians were no longer
to be legally separated on reservations. Instead, "complete integration"
into American society was imposed on them. Fortunately, many people
soon realized termination was a mistake. New laws were passed in the
1960s allowing Indians to be "self-determining"—that is, to govern and
control their own lives within their traditions.

SELECTION FROM
New Mexico Government, THIRD EDITION

Under President Eisenhower (1953–1961) Congress passed termination legislation to end the governmental status of a number of Indian tribes, including, for example, the Menominee tribe of Wisconsin. Several tribes disappeared
as a result of this policy. There was also a related federal policy of "relocation," under which individual Indians and families were encouraged to move
from their reservations into cities, such as Chicago, Los Angeles, Detroit, and
Cincinnati, where they would be helped, with mixed success, to find jobs and
housing. Congress passed Public Law 280, under which certain states (but not
New Mexico) were allowed to assume some jurisdiction over Indian reservations within their boundaries.

Beginning with the administration of President John F. Kennedy, the
Indian policy pendulum began to swing back again, ushering in a period of
self-determination (1961 to the present). . . . Indian tribes were recognized as
permanent governmental units, and Indians would no longer be forced to melt

into the general population. Diversity and the right to be different were increasingly accepted as a part of the American way.

President Lyndon Johnson (1963–69) caused the federal government to pay special attention to the needs of American Indians, particularly because his new antipoverty efforts found them to be the group with the lowest educational levels, the worst health, the poorest housing and employment opportunities, and the lowest family incomes. President Richard Nixon (1969–1974) sent a separate Indian policy message to Congress, in which he declared that American Indians have the right to "self-determination" without "termination." The Menominee tribe was restored to the status of a recognized Indian tribe. Taos Pueblo regained ownership of its 48,000-acre sacred Blue Lake lands from the U.S. Forest Service.

During the 1960s, encouraged by the example of the black civil-rights movement, a pan-Indian rights movement developed in the United States, as Indians began to claim their rights more aggressively. There were some extralegal actions, such as the "Trail of Broken Treaties" takeover of the Bureau of Indian Affairs building in Washington, D.C., in 1972, and the occupation of the village of Wounded Knee on the Pine Ridge Sioux Reservation in South Dakota that same year; but most Indian efforts followed legal courses.

A number of new, more aggressive Indian organizations grew up in the 1970s, around such issues as education, housing, and health. The Council of Energy Resource Tribes (CERT) was formed to assist tribes with the management and control of their own natural resources. The Native American Rights Fund (NARF) became an aggressive advocate of Indian rights. Washington-based national Indian organizations, such as the National Congress of American Indians, NCAI; Americans for Indian Opportunity, AIO; and the National Tribal Chairman's Association, NTCA, continued their representation of Indians and tribes on a broad range of Indian policy issues.

As a result of new Indian solidarity and lobbying, Congress established the American Indian Policy Review Commission, which made specific recommendations for strengthening tribal governments and tribal economies, included Indians as beneficiaries of new civil-rights laws, recognized tribes as sponsoring units of government for new education, housing, and other social programs, and passed a number of important new laws, including the Indian Self-Determination and Education Assistance Act (1975), the Indian Child Welfare Act (1978), the American Indian Religious Freedom Act (1979), and others.

The new assertiveness of American Indians and tribes, generally backed by the national government and the courts, caused something of a white backlash. Groups were formed in some states to press for repeal of Indian treaties and the abolition of the powers of tribal governments. These efforts gained little congressional support, although they continued to be matters of concern to Indians. (Pp. 189–91)

—*Fred Harris and LaDonna Harris*

New Mexico Indian Government

Termination failed and Indian governments became more important. After the 1960s tribes had more freedom. They also had more power. Tribes began to buy more land and start tribal businesses. They also set money aside for scholarships for Indian students.

SELECTION FROM
New Mexico Government, THIRD EDITION

Today the Mescalero Apaches (including those of the Chiricahua, Warm Springs, and Lipan bands who moved there) have a written constitution that provides for an elected tribal council and a separately elected president and vice-president. The Mescaleros have been aggressive in developing a number of business enterprises, including a ski resort and lodge. They were one of the earliest tribes to assert more aggressively their governmental powers concerning taxation, the establishment of tribal courts, and licensing for hunting and fishing on the reservation, irrespective of state laws and requirements. (P. 198)

—*Fred Harris and LaDonna Harris*

Taos Indians Fight for Blue Lake

Indians also became more active in saving their lands. In one case the Taos Indians began a political fight with the United States Forest Service. The fight centered on the pueblo's claim to Blue Lake. Blue Lake lies in the mountains above the pueblo itself. It is surrounded by national forest land.

Blue Lake has always been a sacred place for the Taos Indians. It has been a place where they have worshipped. In the 1930s the national government protected the Taos Indian access to the lake. It gave the Indians a permit to use Blue Lake. It would be their religious shrine. The government also promised to protect the land around the lake from damage.

The permit worked well into the 1960s. Then heavy public use of the national forest damaged the land near Blue Lake. Public use threatened the lake itself. The Taos people again asked the government to protect their rights. As in the 1920s the fight for Indian rights led them to speak out. It drew widespread attention at a time when people nationwide cared about minority rights.

Under much pressure, in late 1970 Congress acted. It set aside Blue Lake for the sole use of the Taos Indians. It also set aside for their use 48,000 acres of the Carson National Forest. Like the fight against the Bursum Bill, New Mexico's Indians had won a great victory.

Indian Economic Life Changes

Some of New Mexico's Indians still earn their living in traditional ways. They farm and raise livestock. In recent years, though, the tribes have developed their own businesses. Chief among them is tourism.

SELECTION FROM
Under the Palace Portal
Native American Artists in Santa Fe

As the bells of Saint Francis Cathedral chime at 7:00 A.M. each day on the Santa Fe plaza, the heart of New Mexico's capital begins to come to life. The shops, galleries, and museums that occupy most of the downtown area will not open for at least two hours, but already there is a bustle of activity along the north side of the plaza. Singly and in small groups, Indian artists walk along the portal, or porch, that fronts the Palace of the Governors, home of the Museum of New Mexico's history museum. Each artist drops a brightly colored cloth, a foam kneeling pad, or a carpet square at a spot along the sidewalk in front of one of the sixty-four numbered spaces that line the wall of the Palace. As the minutes pass cars, trucks, and vans slowly pull up to the curb and other artists emerge and place their cloths along the portal.

Each of the artists has come to the plaza from their homes in the Pueblo villages, on the Indian reservations, or in Albuquerque or Santa Fe for the opportunity to sell the artwork they and their family members have produced as participants in the Native American Vendors Program of the Palace of the Governors. The Portal Program is the most visited program of the Museum of New Mexico and is a central part of Santa Fe's tourism industry.

The more than two million tourists who visit Santa Fe each year make the Portal Program possible, but it is much more than just a market for Indian tourist arts. Growing out of the nearly four-hundred-year history of Santa Fe, the portal market is grounded in centuries of interaction among people from different cultures. It is important to the city in bringing visitors to the plaza area and critically important in the economies of hundreds of Indian families and their communities. The Portal Program is also a central focus of the Indian arts and crafts market in the southwestern United States and plays an important role in promoting Indian arts and in shaping trends in the arts themselves.

Starting in the 1920s, the museum began to host Indian arts and crafts markets to instruct visitors on what constituted "good" (in the eyes of the events' organizers) Indian art and to encourage Indian artists to produce that kind of art instead of hastily made, cheap curios. Over time, the educational emphases of the program have changed.

Museum administrators now emphasize the educational value of the program as residing in the interaction between non-Native visitors and the Indian vendors. Most commonly, visitors learn about the materials and techniques used in the production of Indian jewelry, pottery, and other art forms sold under the portal. Some vendors spend a great deal of time talking to visitors (and potential customers) about their art and about themselves and their communities. On a more basic level, visitors who are unfamiliar with the lives of contemporary Indian people learn a great deal from interacting with the Portal Program participants; they begin to identify Indians as individuals rather than as stereotypes or categories and recognize some of the realities of contemporary Indian life. . . .

But the educational nature of the program goes far beyond what visitors learn about Indian people and the stones, materials, and techniques used in their arts. The Portal Program is educational for vendors too, as it serves to bring together participants with diverse life experiences and from different cultural backgrounds. Native people from urban backgrounds enter the program and learn much from their fellow vendors. Likewise, vendors who have lived their entire lives in Pueblo communities and on reservations learn about the experiences of urban Native people. Young artists who enter the program are gently guided and advised in the development of their art forms by their elders. This mentoring often moves beyond the limits of materials and techniques, and younger vendors are encouraged to learn more about their cultural histories, traditions, and languages. On a more abstract level, the possibility of making a living selling art under the portal not only supports the production of Indian art but also allows artists to live in their home communities and uphold traditional responsibilities that often demand significant time and money. Thus the Portal Program allows New Mexico Native people to maintain their cultural traditions in ways that no other work environment could. . . .

The Portal is a threshold between Indian people and the state of New Mexico. Its very existence depends on a continuing dialogue between and continuing support from both the state museum (and its Board of Regents) and the body of vendors. The Museum of New Mexico continues to define and to defend the program. Without the museum's support, the program would not exist. But at the same time, the program could not exist without the dedication and efforts of the program participants. The vendors and especially the ten-member administrative committee, elected annually by the program membership, ensure that the program continues to operate according to the high standards established by the vendors and the museum. Formal rules and procedures that direct the program are evidence of its place within the bureaucracy of a Western cultural institution; a commitment to giving all interested parties equal voice and to sincere efforts to reach unanimous consensus on issues affecting the program reflect an Indian way of doing things. The Portal Program is an example of cross-cultural cooperation and of how state institutions and indigenous peoples can work together to create programs that are mutually beneficial to participants, the institution, and visitors. . . .

Issues of tradition and authenticity sometimes clash with the desires of artists to expand their modes of expression. Participants must regularly negotiate between producing what tourists want to buy and creating what they themselves see as art, between participating in an ethnic arts and crafts market and fully expressing themselves as creators and innovators. At the same time artists must constantly walk the often thin line between making art rooted in Indian traditions and preserving and protecting those traditions that have often been compromised by both Native and non-Native people.

In 2001, about one thousand Indian artists are registered participants in the Portal Program. Members of Santo Domingo Pueblo make up about one-third of the program; Diné (Navajo) people comprise another one-third. The remaining third includes vendors from nearly all of the other Pueblo villages and tribal groups of New Mexico along with a small number of Hopi people and enrolled members of Indian tribal groups outside New Mexico. To generalize about the vendors is to point out the diversity that exists among them. In addition to coming from many different cultural backgrounds, the vendors have diverse educational, employment, and life histories. Vendors' ages range from the minimum of eighteen to well over eighty, with young people under eighteen often helping in household production or producing their own art to be sold under the portal by their parents or grandparents. On any given day, about an equal number of women and men come to sell. . . .

The Palace portal itself stretches some 259 feet along Palace Avenue, occupying the entire northern side of the Santa Fe plaza. Along the south wall of the Palace, the portal is divided into sixty-four numbered spaces, each twelve bricks wide and six feet deep. The *bancos* (benches) built inside the bastions on each end of the portal hold another two spaces each, and two more spaces are marked along the curb, one on each end of the porch, just inside the bastions. The first space to the west of the main entrance to the Palace (space 34) is reserved for the duty officer of the day. No other spaces are reserved, but starting at 7:00 A.M. vendors may mark desired spaces by placing a cloth or other marker on the sidewalk. Most vendors use the same marker each day, and other vendors can pick who they would like to sit next to for the day through recognition of these markers. If at 8:00 A.M. there are not more vendors than spaces available, each vendor can occupy his or her marked space and begin to set up his or her "cloth" for the day. When more than seventy vendors arrive at the portal before 8:00 A.M., a lottery is held to select spaces for the day. . . .

To become authorized participants in the program, artists must complete application materials, supply a certificate of Indian birth or other proof of tribal membership in a New Mexico tribe, identify a unique maker's mark, and demonstrate their arts for the program committee. Demonstrations are performed at the potential vendors' homes or workshops, which can require significant travel for committee members. Because of the demands on the time and energy of the committee members to observe demonstrations and because of the custom of having at least two observers at each "demo," former committee members and the program coordinator sometimes assist. . . .

While most artists produce pieces with a range of value, and most pieces under the portal are sold for less than $100, artists who produce only low-priced pieces and those who produce few pieces under $100 are all able to support themselves through portal sales. The program is designed to maintain honesty in representation but more important to protect the Indian artists and craftspeople who make up the program. While income for Indian artists is decreasing as imitation work floods the market, the Portal Program provides a place where artists can sell their work to a clientele that appreciates its value.

In discussions of the Native American Vendors Program, issues of authenticity, quality, and what characteristics make objects Indian art surface again and again. The opportunity to buy "real Indian art" from Indian artists is what brings visitors to the portal, and these visitors make participation in the program possible for vendors. But the Portal Program is about much more than these things. It is about multicultural interactions. It is about state institutions and indigenous people working together. It is about the experiences of Indian people in a local, national, and world economy and society. (Pp. 1–13)

—Karl A. Hoerig

The Mescalero Apaches own and operate the Sierra Blanca Ski Area. This ski area is in the Sacramento Mountains in south-central New Mexico. In addition, the Mescaleros own and operate a resort. Their resort's hotel is located three miles south of Ruidoso. Named the Inn of the Mountain Gods, the hotel sits beside a mountain lake. The Jicarilla Apaches, too, have developed tourist sites on their land. These sites are in northwestern New Mexico. They include a lodge at Stone Lake and campgrounds at Dulce and Mundo lakes. The Jicarillas issue permits for fishing, hunting, and camping.

The Navajos, too, have attracted tourists to their reservation. They have also begun a large irrigation project. And they have profited from minerals found on their land. Large companies have leased Navajo land. These companies want to develop the coal, oil, and other resources there.

SELECTION FROM

Native Peoples of the Southwest

The Navajo people are working to improve their economy without destroying their traditional way of life, a challenge that has faced Navajos since the beginning of Anglo contact. . . . Today only a minority of Navajos continue to live off the land with herds of sheep, for most families live in modern houses, many with hogans nearby for ceremonies and, in some cases, for older family members. Members of the extended family often live and work in off-reservation towns but return for weekends and share their income with those who tend the sheep, goats, and cattle. . . .

After World War II renewed interest in the natural resources of the Navajo reservation led companies to discover large oil and gas fields in the Four Corners area. Millions of dollars in oil royalties poured into the tribal treasury, which tribal leaders used to expand tribal government, renovate the police and court system, establish a tribal school program, build new chapter houses, and found the Navajo Forest Products Industry (NFPI) and an electrical distribution system (Navajo Tribal Utilities Authority). Oil companies were the first to begin operations on Navajo land, and forty years later, in the 1960s, coal, vanadium, helium, and uranium companies followed. However, although the fees from leases have enriched the tribal treasury, these fees have constituted a relatively small return for the depletion of this finite resource. Mining has also devastated the landscape. After the removal of coal in the strip-mining process, a vast, open pit remained; only in recent years has the federal government required the restoration of the land. Widespread air pollution resulted from the coal-burning plants, and the water table has dropped dramatically from the diversion of water because of its use as a means of transporting the coal to the plants.

An even more serious health problem came from exposure to uranium mining in the 1970s, when companies paid little attention to the safety of their workers, and when many men and women received high levels of radiation, which resulted in death or debilitating illness. Radioactive materials were so widespread in some areas that unknowingly many families built and lived in homes made of uranium-irradiated materials.

Although the extraction of energy resources is the biggest business in Navajo country, most of the profits from the extraction and processing go to

U.S. corporations rather than to the Navajo. Tribal income from these resources operates government and supplies welfare but does not develop the Navajo economy. Aberle likened the reservation to a colony, because the reservation provides raw materials as well as a market for manufactured goods for the dominant society; only the corporations that exploit the reservation profit while the Navajo people continue to deplete their nonrenewable resources. (Pp. 345–48)

— Trudy Griffin-Pierce

Indians Open Casinos

In the 1990s some Indian tribes looked to gambling casinos to improve their economies. In 1989 Congress passed a law on Indian casinos. The law said tribes could open casinos in a state if gambling was legal there. Since then some 14 tribes have opened casinos in New Mexico. Others, however, chose not to. In 1994 Navajo voters rejected casino gambling.

Casinos have brought changes to the tribes that have them. Casinos have created more jobs on Indian lands. Tribes have used casino money to improve the lives of their members. Casino profits have been used to improve education, medical services, and housing for tribal members. Tribes have used the money to carry out soil conservation projects. Some have also used casino profits to buy more land. Others offer scholarships to their students going to trade schools and colleges. Profits from Indian gaming also help pay for social services once supported by federal programs. Regrettably, though, some people become compulsive gamblers and hurt themselves and others in their lives.

Another positive result, however, has been that many Indian tribes have come together to protect their interests. The National Indian Gaming Association is a lobbying group. It is evidence of how Indians are working together today to protect the policy of self-determination.

CHAPTER EIGHT

Hispanic New Mexicans

World War II Affects Hispanics

New Mexicans were among the first to fight in World War II. After the war started, young Hispanic New Mexicans went to war in large numbers. Other young men and women left New Mexico for the Pacific Coast. There they worked in wartime industries. Many who left came from the villages of northern New Mexico. When the war ended, many never came back. Instead, they stayed in their new homes. One effect of the war, then, was a decline in the population of the villages of northern New Mexico.

After the war, Hispanic veterans continued their education. Under the G.I. Bill for education some went to college. Others went to school to learn trades. Some used skills learned during the war to start their own businesses. Veterans also took advantage of low-cost loans to buy new homes for their families. Also, more and more Hispanics moved to urban areas. They had found it more difficult to earn a living in the rural villages. However, as this trend continued, their older ways of living began to be lost.

Hispanics Have Success

In the years after World War II, the role of Hispanics in New Mexico continued to be important. Their economic power grew. They became leaders in state and national life. In 1996 a United States Census report said that New Mexico has the highest percentage of Hispanic-owned businesses in the nation. The report said that Hispanics owned 21,586 New Mexico businesses out of a total of 107,377. This meant that Hispanics owned

20 percent of all businesses in the state. Texas was second in the number of Hispanic-owned businesses at 12.4 percent. Florida ranked third at 11.8 percent.

At the same time, New Mexico remained a special land for Hispanic political candidates. Here they had long had success. Every year from 1931 to 1997 at least one Hispanic served in Congress. Dennis Chávez served longest, from 1931 to 1962. He won election as both a representative and senator. Chávez used his power to help New Mexico. His work brought military bases and research laboratories to the state. At a national level he joined others to introduce and pass bills that fought discrimination and gave everyone a fair chance to succeed.

SELECTION FROM
Chicano Politics
Reality and Promise, 1940–1990

New Mexico was the only state with a Mexican-American U.S. senator, Dennis Chávez, who served in the Senate from 1935 to 1962. As a Democrat and a member of the New Mexico House of Representatives during the 1920s, Chávez reflected the shift of Mexican-American voters away from the Republican Party. From 1930 to 1935 Chávez served in the U.S. House of Representatives as one of New Mexico's two congressmen. He was reelected to five terms in some bitter and closely contested electoral campaigns; particularly fraught with charges was the election of 1952, which he won by five thousand votes. Arguably, Chávez was the most influential federal official until the late twentieth century. His most memorable interventions involved the establishment of the Fair Employment Practices Committee and the National Labor Relations Act. In foreign relations, he was a strong advocate for mutually benefiting Mexico–United States relations, and he was recognized for this stance by the Mexican government. At his death he was the fourth-ranking member of the Senate; more importantly, he was the most active advocate for Mexican Americans nationally.

In addition to Chávez, New Mexico continued to elect other Mexican Americans to Congress. In 1942, former New Mexico state representative Antonio Fernandez eventually succeeded Chávez in the U.S. House of Representatives. Fernandez, who gained a reputation as an efficient but moderate congressman, was reelected a total of seven times and served until his death from a heart attack in October 1956.

The next *Nuevomexicano* to serve in the U.S. Congress was Democrat Joseph Montoya, descendent of a settler family. The son of a deputy sheriff from Peña Blanca, Sandoval County, and a law school graduate of Georgetown University, he was elected to the House of Representatives in 1957 in a special election to fill Fernandez's former seat. Montoya was first elected to the New Mexico State House of Representatives in 1936, when he was still a law student and too young to be able to vote himself. Eventually, he became Democratic floor leader. From 1941 to 1946, when he served in the New Mexico State Senate, Montoya was the only Mexican-American legislator who did not support a state Fair Employment Practices Committee. Between 1946 and 1951, Montoya served two terms as lieutenant governor of New Mexico. Because of a limitation on two consecutive terms, he served another term as state senator between 1953 and 1954, and he was elected to a third term as lieutenant governor in 1954.

After Montoya's election to the U.S. Congress in 1957, he served in the U.S. House of Representatives until 1964, where he was a member of the influential House Appropriations Committee. Following the death of U.S. Senator Dennis Chávez in 1962, Montoya was viewed by some as his logical successor, and according to the so-called gentlemen's agreement by which one of New Mexico's new U.S. Senators would be a *Nuevomexicano*. However, Anglo-American Republican Governor Edwin L. Mechem, as others before him, did not follow this unwritten agreement and took the U.S. Senate seat. In any case, Montoya was an unusually experienced elected official, and in 1964 he was elected to the Senate; later he was reelected for a second term.

He served on the Appropriations and Public Works committees and on the Select Committee on Small Business. His initial emphasis was consumer protection pertinent to toys, articles, and fabrics; he was best known in the community for his co-authorship of the Bilingual Education Act (1968), for the bill establishing the Cabinet Committee on Opportunities for Spanish-Speaking Americans (1969), and for the resolution initiating the National Hispanic Heritage Week (1976). He played a modest role in Mexico–United States relations, and became a moderate critic of the Vietnam War; but he received the most attention for serving on the Senate committee investigating the Watergate affair.

In 1976 he was defeated for reelection by astronaut Harrison Schmitt, an electoral novice but one who enjoyed great publicity. Moreover, Montoya's base had eroded due to the changing economy and to his own inattentiveness, but also because the type of voter who had supported him previously now came to the polls in fewer numbers. With the election of Republican Manuel Lujan to Congress in 1968, New Mexico had two Mexican-American representatives in Washington, D.C., for a few years. (Pp. 45–47)

—Juan Gómez-Quiñones

Manuel Lujan served as representative from 1969 to 1989. He then became Secretary of the Interior in 1989. Bill Richardson, another Hispanic, represented New Mexicans from 1983 until 1997. He then became United Nations Ambassador. In 1998 he became Secretary of Energy and then governor of New Mexico in 2003. Also at the state level, Hispanics such as Jerry Apodaca and Toney Anaya won elections as governor in the 1970s and 1980s.

Northern New Mexicans Have Problems

While many Hispanics had success, others faced problems. Many who lived in northern villages found it very hard to earn a living. Some who had once had large land grants now were left with small plots of land. Their lands were lost in shady and even illegal actions by some greedy people in the nineteenth century. With the loss of land, many people have lost their old way of life and villages have lost their economic base.

SELECTION FROM

Enchantment and Exploitation
The Life and Hard Times of a New Mexico Mountain Range

The deep lines that furrow Jacobo Romero's face read like a map of the rough country where he has lived his eighty-plus years. He is old enough to remember the day when his father dressed in the suit he reserved for weddings and funerals, drove off with Juan Ortega and the others to hire a lawyer in Santa Fe. His wife, Eloisa, is younger than he and, unlike him, has no recollection of the commotion over the land grant. Her memories of that time revolve instead around the exhilarating terror of a solar eclipse, and the way the rough wooden floor of the Trampas Church used to hurt her knees during mass.

Together they look back over the intervening years like sailors who have landed in a place so different from where they started that comparing one to the other makes both sound implausibly exotic.

When they were young, the Hispanic villages of the Sangres were a separate world where it was extremely rare for anyone to see a gringo, let alone talk to one. Now the old couple have several for sons-in-law. In the days of their youth, Spanish was the only language they heard spoken, but now a majority of their grandchildren and great-grandchildren speak mainly English, and many speak it with the same urbane inflections one hears on television. Other old people in the mountain villages have found these changes demoralizing and painful, but not these two. They travel from one end of the country to the other to visit their children, and they find the present to be as satisfactory as the past. Still, they say, there is no denying that much of value has been lost. They consider themselves fortunate to have known the old days when the mountain villages were self-contained and neatly self-sufficient, and when life, moving at a horse-drawn pace, had all the stability—and hardship— of the mountains themselves. . . .

The mountain villages of the old days were hardly idyllic. Frequent dry spells during the growing season produced heated arguments about the management of the irrigation ditches, many of them fanned by bitter, long-standing feuds. . . . Misunderstanding and narrow-mindedness could sour a man's life, and the habit of thinking about the outside world could as easily bring him to grief or save him from it. Yet for all their faults, the villages possessed an integrity and unity that is altogether lacking in most modern communities. . . .

The villagers lived in isolation from the outside world and drew on local resources for the things they required. On foundations of mud and river cobbles, they laid up the walls of their houses with sun-dried adobe bricks and mud mortar. Their roof beams and lintels they cut from the surrounding forest; their ceilings were herringbone arrangements of sapling poles overlaid with brush, leaves, and ultimately a thick layer of dirt; and for plaster inside and out they used more of their one inexhaustible resource—mud, sometimes dressing up the final coat with the addition of sparkling micaceous sand. From these humble materials they obtained a house that, although prone to leak and always hard to clean, was warm in winter and cool in summer. Moreover, it had a gently organic, sculptural quality: every window and door opening had smooth, hand-rounded edges; walls were not quite plane, and their modest undulations gave them a fluid grace in spite of their great thickness and bulk. The house belonged to the landscape as truly as the tan dirt of the yard before it or the weed that grew in its roof. When it was abandoned and no one any longer repaired its walls with fresh plaster or shoveled its roof free of snow, the entire structure returned to the soil as completely as it had once come from it. . . .

The old people of the villages remember the days of self-sufficiency with pride. At least in memory, the poverty they experienced was tolerable. Every man was his own master and the equal of his neighbors. Although manufactured goods were scarce, no one went hungry. There was always plenty of lamb to eat, as well as mutton and goat and sometimes venison from a deer that the dogs chased and exhausted in a winter snowdrift. There were wild turkeys, many more than today, and chicken, pork, beef, trout from the river, grouse, and rabbit. People were poor in material comforts and their children slept crowded together, several to the bed, but they were rich in what they valued most: time, family, and the freedom of the land.

There was extravagance in the old customs that the villagers' ancestors had brought up the trail from Mexico. Several times a year each community held protracted celebrations of feasts and saint's days. One of the most important was the feast of the patron saint of the village, when the santo, the statue representing him, was taken from the church and carried at the head of a procession to every corner of the village to bless the fields, the irrigation ditches, and the ditch gates. Although their feeling for the mountains and mesas that enclosed them may not have been as profoundly religious as that of their Pueblo neighbors, the Hispanic villagers showed in this custom a deep reverence for the land of the village itself. . . .

Besides common sense, the only defense of the villagers against pain and sickness was their extensive herbal lore, much of it borrowed from the Pueblos. Herbs were credited with help against every ailment from cancer to the pangs of love. As everywhere else in the world, the medicinal use of herbs, which is still common in northern New Mexico, was a mixture of both real curing and elaborate superstition. One of the most frequently used native plants was *oshá* (*Ligusticum porteri*), a member of the celery family, which grows several feet tall in the moist meadows of the high country. In various preparations the root of the *oshá* plant appears to be genuinely effective in soothing a variety of stomach troubles, and the leading herbalist in Santa Fe says that even today he cannot keep enough of the plant in stock. . . .

Today the people of northern New Mexico still lack a viable economic base, and they still depend heavily on government assistance. The small farms of the villages produce some hay and beef, both of which are readily converted into cash, but only a handful of villagers earn a substantial part of their living from agriculture. In order to make ends meet, many villagers find jobs with the Forest Service, the school system, or the construction trades, but there are never enough jobs to go around. The Hispanos of the southern Sangres are among the poorest people in the United States. In 1970 nearly 60 percent of the residents of Mora County lived in what the federal government officially defined as poverty. For Rio Arriba, San Miguel, and Taos counties, which are also predominantly Hispanic, the figure ranged between 34 and 40 percent. Nationally fewer than 11 percent of American families belonged to that category. . . .

Because economic prospects were so bleak in the years after World War II, vast numbers of young people left the villages and moved to such urban centers as Albuquerque, Denver, and Los Angeles. They left behind scores of boarded-up houses and decaying barns, and their departure depleted the villages of both skills and leadership. . . .

The exodus from the mountain villages was never a joyful one, for there was nothing in the cities to replace the beauty and the strong community ties of the mountain world. Unfortunately, the conditions that caused the exodus have still not changed, and few young people who stay in the villages escape chronic unemployment. Understandably, many of them are bitter about their fate. They know that their land grants were taken from them by Anglo outsiders, and many of them further blame their poverty on other unfriendly Anglo influences and institutions, including the Forest Service. Beginning in the late 1960s they began to espouse the political and cultural goals of Mexican-Americans throughout the Southwest and to flex their political muscle under the slogan of *Chicano Power*. The new consciousness led to the establishment of various village clinics and cooperative economic ventures, as well as to numerous stormy political confrontations. Whether it will lead further, as many hope, to new social and economic vitality for northern New Mexico remains to be seen. (Pp. 193–212)

—*William deBuys*

To survive, the Hispanics of northern New Mexico often raised cattle. They grazed their cattle on national forest land. As the years passed, however, the United States Forest Service allowed fewer cattle on public lands. The northern New Mexicans saw this as a threat to their way of life.

So, many of them rallied behind a new leader. The time was the mid 1960s. The leader was Reies López Tijerina. He promised to help northern New Mexicans.

The Alianza Is Formed

A newcomer to New Mexico, Tijerina was a preacher. He soon began to speak out about the problems of his new home. He talked about the loss of land by Hispanic New Mexicans. He talked about a loss of community spirit. To solve these problems, Tijerina argued that Hispanics needed to unite. He said they should work for equal rights.

In his fight for equal rights, Tijerina formed a new group. This was the *Alianza Federal de Mercedes*. This means the Federal Alliance of Land Grants. Known best as the *Alianza*, the group grew quickly. It had at its peak perhaps as many as 5,000 members.

Tijerina claimed that *Alianza* members rightfully owned millions of acres of land. The land in question was forest service and Anglo-American ranch land. This land, he said, belonged to *Alianza* members because of their land grant titles. The *Alianza* and its leader got a great deal of national attention in the 1960s. Again the public was aware of the struggle for minority rights.

This attention grew in the fall of 1966. In October Tijerina and 350 supporters took direct action. They moved into the national forest northwest of Abiquiu. They seized control of Echo Amphitheater, a natural formation within the forest. They then announced the birth of a new country. This country was located, Tijerina said, on a Spanish land grant.

Forest rangers went to the occupied land. When they arrived, Tijerina and his followers arrested the forest rangers. They charged the rangers with trespassing. These moves brought the *Alianza* much news coverage.

A raid on the courthouse of Tierra Amarilla gained the group even more publicity. The raid occurred in June 1967. It included a shoot-out. As a result, two officers of the law were wounded. This time state officials responded. With the governor absent, the lieutenant governor sent the state's national guard into Rio Arriba County. Equipped with tanks, the guardsmen arrested some *Alianza* members. However, most of those involved in the raid escaped.

As for Tijerina, he stood trial for his part in the courthouse raid.

He defended himself in court in grand style. The jury ruled in his favor. Tijerina later stood trial in federal court for his role in occupying national forest land. He faced charges of destroying government property. This time the jury found him guilty. Tijerina spent more than two years in a federal prison in El Paso.

Tijerina failed in his land grant fight. No lands were returned to the villagers of northern New Mexico. He also lost support after the raid on Tierra Amarilla. Still, Tijerina had caught the attention of young Hispanics. He and his followers had voiced the hopes of many New Mexicans. He also focused attention on the U.S. government's role in taking over land in New Mexico. Such actions had hurt other people, too.

SELECTION FROM
New Mexico
An Interpretive History

In the year 1922, the small Indian pueblo of Tesuque eight miles north of Santa Fe closed its doors to the outside world and prepared to starve in protest to the Bursum Bill then pending in Congress. In the year 1957, a crusty rancher named John Prather took up his rifle to defend his land from the United States government, which wanted to add it to the White Sands Missile Range. In the year 1966, a band of armed Hispanos invaded the Echo Amphitheater Park in northern New Mexico, administered by the National Forest Service, and declared it to be the free and independent Republic of San Joaquin. Three events wholly unrelated, it would seem. But were they?

It is doubtful that the participants—Indian, Anglo, and Hispano—in each of these incidents saw beyond the small circle of their own immediate troubles and perceived that they had become enmeshed in a larger problem inherent in the workings of the democratic process. That problem, foundation-cracking in its implications, was one that worried founders of the republic and has continued to perplex just men to the present day. And it is this: how can individuals and minorities be protected in their basic freedom and rights if an overbearing majority chooses to mistreat them? Beginning with the Bill of Rights, successive laws were formed to curb despotic tendencies on the part of government (which enforces the will of the majority) and to maintain a climate in which personal initiative and the creative impulse could thrive. . . .

The Pueblo Indians' fight against the Bursum Bill, John Prather's private war to keep his ranch, and the Hispanos' Republic of San Joaquin (founded as part of a continuing struggle to recover lost land grants)—all were expressions of the view that the little man in a democracy has a right to be heard and to survive. These three cases are singled out, because in each one people were ready to lay their lives on the line for what they believed.

The struggle of the Pueblo people to maintain their islands of individuality and culture in the great sea of conforming pressures that twentieth-century America had become reached a point of crisis when New Mexico's Senator Holm O. Bursum in 1922 introduced his congressional bill. That measure was designed to settle the claims of white squatters on Pueblo land. But in doing so it largely ignored the Indians' claims to the land. When the full details of the Bursum Bill became known, the Pueblos and their friends in the white community mounted a full-scale attack upon it, creating a controversy that soon gained nationwide attention. . . .

The heated debate over the Bursum Bill had aroused broad interest in Indian rights and had focused attention on New Mexico and its people, as well. Even more fundamental was the shift in government policy that ultimately resulted. Before the affray, the Bureau of Indian Affairs had actively worked to discredit the culture and religion of the first Americans and to bring about their speedy assimilation. Now, with the defeat of the bill and clear evidence of widespread support for the Indians' effort to maintain their tribal integrity, a more tolerant attitude began to make itself felt among government policy-makers and administrators. . . .

[Almost two decades later, citizens throughout New Mexico were united by the United States' entry into World War II.] In proportion to the scant population, New Mexicans—Indian, Hispano, and Anglo alike—experienced the highest casualty rate of any state during the opening years of the conflict. Two of their regiments were at Bataan in the Philippines, and after Bataan fell to the Japanese, they endured the infamous "Death March" and three years of imprisonment. Some of the survivors, keeping a vow made during that harrowing time, later undertook a pilgrimage on foot to the rustic adobe Santuario de Chimayó, a popular Hispano shrine north of Santa Fe that dates from colonial days.

Another course of events during the war was to make an even deeper impression on New Mexico and at the same time would start John Prather on the road to his small rebellion. . . .

The explosion of the atomic bomb at the White Sands Proving Ground (now the White Sands Missile Range) was felt over much of New Mexico in that summer of 1945. But it was what followed that proved more disturbing to the residents of the Tularosa Basin. The military was in need of land, a great deal of it, for the testing of rockets and the training of their crews, a program deemed crucial for national defense. To expand the range, hundreds of thousands of acres were ordered withdrawn from the public domain and from private ownership, which meant condemnation proceedings were instituted against surrounding ranchers. Many of these people waged fierce court battles and appeared at congressional hearings in a bid to keep their land, but one by one, over succeeding years, they lost out and were displaced.

Then, in 1955, the government, as it crept eastward toward the Sacramento Mountains swallowing up chunks of ground in whale-sized gulps, ran straight into eighty-two-year-old John Prather. His land, which he had held and worked for fifty years, was not for sale, Prather announced. And anyone who tried to put him off might get hurt. In the U.S. District Court at Albuquerque, a condemnation suit resulted in a ninety-day eviction notice for John Prather and his neighbors. The old man's response to that action was to issue a public statement: "I'm going to die at home."

The army found itself in an awkward position. Prather, with all his stubbornness and independence, was an authentic pioneer who had a personal hand in taming the West. He was a survivor of that frontier stock whose experience had come to be viewed by Americans in romantic and heroic terms. If he stood by his guns, as he was threatening to do, the whole affair might be ballyhooed to the skies by the news-hungry press and the army made to look like an oppressive monster. The situation demanded gentleness and tact, and government officials mustered every ounce of that they could. . . .

Public opinion was clearly swinging to the side of the courageous old rancher, and since he could not be moved, short of force, a directive from Washington ordered military personnel to withdraw from the Prather Ranch. The army then went back to court and obtained a new writ exempting the ranch house and fifteen surrounding acres from confiscation; the remainder of the land was forthwith annexed to the military reservation. If John Prather raised no further fuss, he would be left alone.

That ended the matter. Prather had lost his ranch, but he had also won a victory of sorts. Standing firm, he had forced the U.S. government to compromise and in so doing had chiseled himself a niche in the history of southern New Mexico. As one writer later explained it, John Prather reacted as his forebears had reacted against invasion of their independence and property rights. His was the code and the psychology of the 1880s, and he was the last of his kind.

The upheaval in New Mexico produced by World War II, by the growth of postwar defense installations and industries, and by the sudden influx of population—all of which hastened the end of John Prather's world—also contributed to rising social and economic problems among Hispanos in the mountains of the north. Again, as in the cases of the Pueblo Indians and the ranchers of the Tularosa Basin, a struggle for land became the focus of a human drama, bringing private citizens into conflict with established authority. . . .

In the forefront of those who profited from [land title claims awaiting settlement] were the lawyers—the class of men who Father Martínez had predicted in the 1850s would supplant priests as the real power in New Mexico. For clearing titles, they exacted huge fees. These fees were usually paid in land from that held in common, so that, within time, as seemingly endless litigation over titles continued, sharp-eyed American lawyers and their associates acquired possession of prodigious sections of the Spanish grants. One Santa Fe attorney, for example, was reported by a local newspaper in 1894 to have an interest in seventy-five grants and to own outright nearly two million acres. . . .

Unfamiliar with Spanish law protecting and preserving village commons, American judges had ruled that the ancient common lands could be partitioned and divided among the numerous grant-claimants. That meant that vast areas of upland pastures and mountain woods, of which villagers had made free use for generations, were now allotted to individuals who could put them up for sale if they chose. Not surprisingly, surrounding lands soon slipped from the grasp of community members and passed to the control of outsiders—often cattlemen from Texas—or into the public domain, where much of it was placed under the National Forest Service. A similar pattern of land loss was experienced by a number of American Indian tribes in the twentieth century, when by Congressional Act their reservations were broken up and the land granted in severalty, thereby destroying the common-property base of community existence. . . .

As the 1970s opened, land problems and poverty continued to plague northern New Mexico—the "Appalachia of the Southwest," some observers had labeled it. However, numerous federal programs and a renewed willingness on the part of Hispanos of all ages to work for the revitalization of village culture gave promise of a more productive future. As yet, however, New Mexico's distinctive Hispanic heritage has not received the recognition and respect that it deserves as one of America's oldest and most creative wells of human experience. Whether that error will ever be fully corrected remains to be seen. . . .

What now seems clear to all thoughtful New Mexicans is that they must keep looking for ways to preserve the old alongside the new. And in the face of diminishing resources, they must seek to perpetuate some measure of that reverence for the land and its waters that was characteristic of the best among both Spanish and Anglo-American pioneers and among the original Indian inhabitants. (Pp. 168–89)

—*Marc Simmons*

Cultural Pride Grows

New Mexico's Hispanic heritage has always served to anchor its people in their traditions. But in the 1960s and 1970s, a new understanding of heritage emerged. This became the Chicano and Chicana Movement. It brought a growth in cultural pride.

SELECTION FROM
The Contested Homeland
A Chicano History of New Mexico

Nowhere in the United States has the presence of Chicanos and Chicanas been more evident than in New Mexico. Since the territorial period (1848) and after statehood (1912) they have represented a larger percentage of the total population than in any other state. *Nuevomexicano*s comprised the first major settlement in the northern periphery of Mexico, and they have remained a vital, culturally identifiable group for several centuries. A substantial number of families can trace their ancestry to seventeenth-century settlers, many of whom belonged to the colonial oligarchy of the province.

Numerous villages and cities, among them Mora, Los Lunas, Madrid, Los Padillas, and Los Griegos, carry the names of these early settlers, and pride in Spanish descent runs deep. Identification with a Spanish past is clearly stronger in New Mexico than in other regions that have a strong Chicano presence.

Early in its development there emerged in New Mexico an influential and well-to-do Hispanic elite that set the structural and social parameters of the region. This group managed to retain its privilege and after 1848, it shared power with Anglo-Americans. In no other region in the country has a Chicano elite wielded as much power and influence as in New Mexico. In all walks of life—politics, education, labor, business, and cultural production—this elite has functioned as an influential pressure group that has greatly impacted the institutions and social interactions in the state. Self-determination, resistance, and cultural maintenance are repeated themes in the *Nuevomexicano* historical experience and legacy. From the Anglo-American invasion of 1846 to the end of the millennium, the *Nuevomexicano* community has struggled valiantly and with a certain degree of success to maintain its traditions, language, land holdings, political participation, ethnic identity, and individual way of life. Either collectively or individually, using legal or extralegal measures, *Nuevomexicano*s have struggled against the forces of colonialism, ethnocentrism, racism, and sexism throughout their history. Because of their numbers, class composition, percentage of the population, and extensive political representation and experience, they have more than survived or endured. They have triumphed and still maintain a dominant *Nuevomexicano* presence and influence in all facets and regions of the state. In fact, Anglos frequently have had to adjust their assumptions and practices to local ways. (Pp. 1–2)

—*Erlinda Gonzales-Berry and David R. Maciel*

A Culture Recorded

As life changed after World War II, some New Mexicans began to preserve the special history and culture of Hispanics. Historian Fray Angélico Chávez collected and retold their history.

SELECTION FROM
Fray Angélico Chávez
Poet, Priest, and Artist

Beginning in the 1940s, Fray Angélico began to systematically research the roots of the Hispano presence in New Mexico. Although not an academically trained historian, Chávez brought a rigorous and meticulous quality to his investigations. . . .

Accepting the responsibility for historical accuracy Chávez sought to understand and to educate himself as well as others about the non-Anglo, Hispano roots of New Mexico's history. Having not learned about this past either at home or in school, Chávez felt—and believed that those whom he called native New Mexicans did also—a certain historical vacuum or ambivalence at a time of increased Anglo-American influence in the post–World War II era.

Chávez approached the excavation of Hispanos' roots with a fervor and discipline that conveyed his religious commitment as a Franciscan. In a sense, he became a historical missionary. History, especially the role of the Hispano Church, would bring new spiritual and cultural nourishment to his people.

Chávez's historical pilgrimage became both a personal as well as a collective endeavor. Of this connection between the personal and the collective in his work, Father Thomas Steele has written concerning *My Penitente Land*, Fray Angélico's most autobiographical historical text, "Chávez's book embodies *Chávez's* New Mexico, '*my* penitente land': his personally appropriated New Mexico, the New Mexico that formed him into the man he is, the New Mexico that is profoundly and vastly more his than it is anybody else's." Chávez himself acknowledged his personal identification with the Hispano roots of New Mexico: "I myself was born when those first Spanish settlers were preparing to enter New Mexico, their land and mine. A goodly number of them are my own proven direct ancestors, some by several lines."

If history was a way to understand one's own genealogy it was also a way of providing a collective identity. For example, in his important work on tracing the origins of New Mexican Hispano families, Fray Angélico provided a sense not only of roots but perhaps more importantly of subjectivity—of being somebody. Chávez believed that Hispanos and non-Hispanos needed to know the Spanish-surname background of Hispano families as well as the place names that derived from Spanish names. *Origins of New Mexico Families: A Genealogy of the Spanish Colonial Period*, first published in 1954, represents a form of "collective biography." It gives attention to the stories of the various Hispano family lines from the seventeenth century to the mid-nineteenth century. This includes families such as the Armijos, the Vigils, the Vargases, and, of course, the Chávezes. Fray Angélico, never fully accepting what one writer called the "Spanish Fantasy," noted that while many of these initial families had migrated to New Mexico in hopes of achieving social status as hidalgos, most were of modest military and pastoral backgrounds: "good folks in the main, who were neither peons nor convicts." But what particularly impressed Fray Angélico was how closely knit these kinships were. In effect, he saw colonial Hispano settlements as family or at least extended family.

Part of Fray Angélico's search for personal and collective historical roots involved countering the view from Anglo-America of native New Mexicans, both Indians and Hispanos, as being the "other": of not being truly American, and of possessing a culture including religious practices that did not conform to an Anglo-American standard. Chávez opposed these biased and even racist opinions by stressing the deep roots of Hispanos in an area that became part of the United States.

Fray Angélico believed in an inclusive rather than an exclusive American history. Displaying what the historian of the Southwest Herbert Eugene Bolton called the concept of "Greater America," Chávez, at the risk of uncritically examining the role of the Spanish conquering expeditions into New Mexico, nevertheless used these *entradas*—including that of Coronado in 1540—to emphasize the long-standing Hispanic presence in the region. This was looking at American history from a south-to-north perspective, opposing the standard narrative that American history begins with the thirteen original colonies. Chávez revised or attempted to revise this interpretation by integrating the Spanish colonies that antedated the first English settlements. In this version, Coronado is just as American as John Smith.

In seeking the historical roots of New Mexico from the perspective of religion, Fray Angélico further asserted the Hispanic character of the area by ascribing a sacredness to it. Like Chicano movement activists who linked the concept of *Aztlán* (the mythical pre-Columbian roots of the Southwest) to that of sacred space, Chávez interpreted Hispanic New Mexico in a similar vein. Comparing New Mexico to other parts of the United States, Fray Angélico wrote, "But the New Mexican landscape has something that they all lack. It is Holy Land." The Rio Grande in Chávez's narrative becomes the River Jordan. Religion or sacredness permeated New Mexico.

Fray Angélico noted that many towns and geographic sites possessed religious names. In his work on New Mexican religious place names, he countered the tendency by Anglos to dehistoricize the landscape pertaining to the pre-American period. It is this religiosity or sacredness that he believed to be at the heart of New Mexico's early Hispanic past—religiosity that not only reinforced Fray Angélico's own personal devotion to the Church but also gave this history its special quality.

Through his research in early Church documents and in his impressive annotation of the archives of the Archdiocese of Santa Fe from 1678 to 1900, Chávez documented the origins of American history in New Mexico. He was saying that New Mexico and its native Hispano population possessed a history because they could document it. Here the role of the Church as the guardian of historical identity was crucial.

The religious nature of this history validated for Fray Angélico the Hispano experience. To him, religion was synonymous with ethnicity at a time (the 1940s and 1950s) when it was not particularly acceptable to be "ethnic" or to assert in any oppositional manner one's ethnic identity, a time one scholar has called the "Age of Consensus." This is not to say that Chávez was simply using religion to discuss ethnicity but rather that for him religion and ethnicity in the case of New Mexico's colonial history were one and the same. "One can only feel the highest admiration for the majority of the padres," he concluded, "who kept the missions going in the face of either poverty and loneliness, and for the Hispanic folk who for generations had survived among perils and hardship that might have driven other people to desertion, if not extinction."

In this search for roots, Fray Angélico clearly did not believe that the clock could be moved back. As with other native New Mexican writers there is in Chávez's writings a touch of nostalgia, but there is also a realistic awareness that well into the twentieth century many new changes had taken place. "We can't turn history back," he noted, "no matter how many efforts are now being made to remedy old injustices." Indeed, it was precisely these transformations, such as the growing acculturation of Hispanos, that motivated Fray Angélico's search for history. He sensed a loss of historical identity and lamented it. Lack of identity disempowered Hispanos in a land that bore so much of their imprint. To empower Hispanos, Fray Angélico embarked on a crusade to regain this self-awareness. This was not nostalgia but a struggle to combat prejudice and the perceived loss of religious fervor among native New Mexicans. Historical consciousness, for Chávez, was the remedy for achieving equality and regaining one's soul. (Pp. 27–30)

—*Mario T. García*

And in 1972 a private group opened El Rancho de las Golondrinas. Located near Santa Fe, this became a "living history museum." There visitors can view Spanish colonial ways of living. New Mexicans also celebrate Hispanic New Mexico History Month each April.

In the 1980s Hispanic artists and the Hispanic Culture Foundation began a much larger project. After years of hard work, they were successful. In 2000 the National Hispanic Cultural Center opened. Located in Albuquerque, the center has several functions. These are to preserve and promote the arts, culture, and history of Hispanic peoples around the world.

SELECTION FROM

Santa Fe Hispanic Culture
Preserving Identity in a Tourist Town

In the year 2000, no large differences of perceptions existed between Hispanic and non-Hispanic Santa Feans regarding the characteristics that they believed defined local Hispanic culture. There were concerns voiced that the local Hispanic culture needed to be protected and nurtured in order to be preserved, and that it was in danger of being diminished or lost if steps were not taken to maintain it.

In personal interviews with Santa Fe cultural leaders, educators, and historians, several themes emerged with regard to Santa Fe Hispanic culture. Several interviewees commented that the Santa Fe Hispanic culture was continually in a state of transformation but that change was not something to be feared. Historian Orlando Romero stated that the culture was "very much alive, but in transition." Tom Chávez, director of the National Hispanic Cultural Center, emphasized that "strong cultures embrace outside influences" and he commented, "My fear is that we don't try to freeze the culture in a place and time because that will kill it." Rudolfo Anaya, acclaimed New Mexican author, and Father Jerome Martínez y Alire mirrored these sentiments in their interviews with *Crosswinds Weekly*. Anaya stated that cultures were "organic and constantly changing." Martínez y Alire said, "Native Hispanic culture has always been evolving." Roberto Mondragon, a Santa Fe political and educational leader, and Ana Pacheco, publisher of *La Herencia*, both emphasized the importance of the Spanish language for maintaining Santa Fe Hispanic culture. Pacheco called the Spanish language "the glue that keeps the culture together." Romero and Mondragón emphasized the importance of Catholicism in Santa Fe Hispanic cultural self-identity. Chávez and Romero both commented on the unique character of Santa Fe because of its isolation from Spain and Mexico during the early years of its founding in the 1600s and 1700s.

Information gathered in these personal interviews with Santa Fe residents and leaders gives a snapshot of the characteristics of Santa Fe Hispanic culture. . . . Just as Santa Fe Hispanos differ in the labels they prefer (Hispanic, Latino, etc.), they have a variety of perspectives with regard to what defines their culture. As Orlando Romero commented, "Santa Fe Hispanic culture is not easily defined."

The Fiesta de Santa Fe as the major Hispanic cultural festival in Santa Fe is in many ways a barometer of local Hispanic cultural identity. As Elizabeth Rosa Lovato, 1999 Fiesta queen, stated, "Fiesta is not a celebration of conquest to me; it's a celebration of culture." The Fiesta serves as a means of reinforcing and communicating Santa Fe Hispanic self-identity. It is a touchstone for many Santa Fe Hispanos who define the celebration as a source of cultural pride and unity and prefer not to emphasize any of the negative connotations associated with the reconquest of Santa Fe in 1692–1693. . . . As the 1999 Don Diego de Vargas of the Fiesta, Tommy Trujillo, stated, "Taking classes for ten years wouldn't give me as much knowledge of my culture."

The Fiesta reflects many of the most important aspects of Santa Fe Hispanic culture. Religious faith in the form of the Fiesta masses and the prominence of La Conquistadora are central to the celebration. Language, ancestry and heritage, the arts, food, and connection to "place" are all celebrated during the Santa Fe Fiesta. Even though the Fiesta is touted as a community event for Santa Feans of all backgrounds, many aspects are strongly influenced by the local Hispanic culture.

Ironically, even the Santa Fe Fiesta, the main Hispanic cultural celebration in the city, is heavily influenced by the Anglo culture in a variety of ways.

The Santa Fe Fiesta is both a self-defined and other-defined cultural festival for Santa Fe Hispanics. The merging of the Santa Fe Fiesta and Fourth of July celebrations in 1883 for the Tertio-Millennial Exposition was the beginning of Anglo influence on the Fiesta. This influence increased in 1919 when the Museum of New Mexico and its mainly Anglo staff revived the Fiesta. Over the years, Anglo contributions to the Santa Fe Fiesta have included the Historical/Hysterical Parade, the introduction of a Fiesta queen and De Vargas role, the Children's Pet Parade, and of course Zozobra, who is sacrificed each Fiesta. . . .

Santa Fe Hispanic cultural self-identity is unavoidably influenced by the fact that Santa Fe is a tourist town in which local culture and local history have been made into commodities for sale by the tourism industry. The issue of cultural identity formation transmitted by members of an individual's own cultural group (self-defined identity) or by people and cultures outside of the individual's cultural group (other-defined identity) is of particular importance in this environment.

The question of how each identity has affected the other is a complex issue. The push since the early 1900s to promote Santa Fe as a tourist haven has redefined Hispanic culture from the early Anglo-American perception of it as inferior and backward to a new definition of Santa Fe Hispanic culture as exotic and romantic. The Hispanic people of Santa Fe have simultaneously rejected and internalized these other-defined stereotypes to differing degrees during the past century. The state museum system has generally provided a more balanced picture of Hispanic history and identity than commercial interests, allowing those with the interest and motivation to explore Hispano culture in a more realistic fashion.

The challenge of trying to maintain and understand cultural self-identity in a tourist mecca is not unique to Santa Fe. This struggle occurs with native Hawaiians, Chinese San Franciscans, and other ethnic groups worldwide. The struggle between self-defined and other-defined cultural identity is intensified as old traditions and customs fall away in an ever-more homogenized world. Mass cultural views infiltrate native cultures, making their members susceptible to accepting simplified stereotypes of themselves and their own culture. These cultural pressures often cause anger and resentment for some within the culture as they try to hold on to their own authentic cultural identity apart from commerce and tourism concerns. These concerned natives protest that their culture does not exist simply for the benefit and enjoyment of others. For example, Santa Fe Hispanics have often voiced resentment about the transformation of the Santa Fe Plaza from a community meeting place to a tourist-shopping venue. They wonder if Santa Fe exists primarily for its native inhabitants or as a playground for outsiders.

A key question is: At what point do the stereotypes and myths surrounding a culture become the reality? All cultures to a certain extent can be said to be in many ways "mythical creations." What may be important is not so much that cultures contain myth but rather who "controls" the development and the perpetuation of these myths. Is it the "inside" group or the "other" that holds the influence? This issue is one of power and self-determination. The question may be asked: Who defines the culture in question? When looking at the issue of authenticity versus invented traditions, people often create reality and invent language to reinforce their perspective.

Santa Fe's cultural landscape has gone through many perceptual shifts during its history. An example was the view following the U.S. occupation in 1846 that Santa Fe's adobe architecture was backward and undesirable. This perception began to change in the 1900s, and today adobe construction in the city is considered the most prestigious. "Santa Fe style" furnishings, art, clothing, and various other goods are all artifacts of an invented cultural tradition. Even the historical revisionism of the "bloodless" reconquest of Santa Fe that is celebrated during the annual Santa Fe Fiesta is an example of shifts in viewpoints that have taken place in the city throughout its history.

No wonder that confusion exists in regard to cultural self-identity for Santa Fe Hispanics who live in a city in which the definition of their culture is continually shifting and transforming. (Pp. 122–28)

—Andrew Leo Lovato

PART THREE

New Mexico Today

Introduction

You know that New Mexico became a state in 1912. If you stay in New Mexico long enough, though, you will find out that many Americans do not know this. One Albuquerque family found this out in 1994.

That summer the husband tried to buy tickets to World Cup soccer games in Los Angeles. He talked to the ticket agent and asked that the tickets be mailed to him in New Mexico. The ticket agent replied, "We cannot mail tickets to a foreign country." A month later the wife visited New York. She wanted to make a collect phone call home to report on her trip. After a pause, the operator said, "I have to switch you to someone else. I cannot place an international collect call."

The following winter their daughter stood beside a pay phone at Angel Fire, New Mexico. She overheard a young skier from Texas tell his mother, "I don't think they will take those pesos I brought here." Who New Mexicans are and what New Mexico is still escapes many people.

In this part you will read about how many New Mexicans there are today and what problems they face. You will learn about some of the modern artists and painters. You will also learn how New Mexicans celebrate their past alongside the present. And finally, you will review what New Mexico's history has to teach us.

CHAPTER NINE

Growth and Issues

New Mexico Grows

Today there are more New Mexicans than ever. In 2000 the Census Bureau found 1,810,046 people living here. Sixty years before there had been 531,818. Since 1940, then, the state's population had more than tripled. New Mexicans having children accounts for some of the growth. The rest moved here from other places.

The 1950s saw the fastest growth. Some people came to work at military bases. Others came to work in weapons research. Military bases helped towns like Clovis and Alamogordo grow. Los Alamos and also Albuquerque grew because of scientific and weapons research. Meanwhile, oil and gas booms drew still others to southeastern New Mexico. The state was changing rapidly. The cultural traditions became more varied and complex, too.

SELECTION FROM
Contemporary New Mexico, 1940–1990

New Mexico is a unique land. Both long-time residents and first-time visitors agree on that. But exactly where does the uniqueness lie? Here there is no agreement. The most common interpretation has been that of the "Three Cultures." It is the presence of the Indian, Hispanic, and "Anglo-Pioneer" cultures, this argument goes, that accounts for New Mexico's distinctive qualities. Many an early twentieth-century study suggested that all three blended in easy harmony. But a 1993 analysis is a bit more cautious, suggesting that "although the three cultures intermingle, they never completely blend."

During the past half-century, New Mexicans have had to confront several new "cultures." In turn, these cultures have fostered, overlapped, blended with, and at times, transformed the "heroic triad" of New Mexico's ancient past.

The first new "culture" is the culture of landscape. From the frying-pan flatness of the Llano Estacado to the alpine beauty of the northern mountains, New Mexico's landforms have ever inflamed the imagination. Modern scientists have counted six of the seven climate zones in the state. The land of New Mexico has always been a source of wonder.

While the landforms themselves have changed little in centuries, the landscape itself has altered considerably. After the war, the federal government withdrew millions of acres to create military bases and missile ranges in Clovis, Albuquerque, Alamogordo, and Roswell. Increased regulations by the National Forest Service, National Park Service, Bureau of Land Management, and various state agencies became a fact of life. Simultaneously, as easy access to public lands diminished, the state population increased steadily. . . .

Second is the culture of "big science." Although New Mexico hosted its share of astronomers, physicians, and anthropologists before World War II, big science began in earnest in the fall of 1942. As the most crucial cog in the sprawling Anglo-American Manhattan Project, the Los Alamos scientists wrestled with a momentous assignment: to produce an atomic weapon to end World War II "in the shortest possible time."

The atomic age began at 5:30 A.M., July 16, 1945, at the strangely named "Trinity Site," about thirty-five miles east of Socorro. From that moment forward, New Mexico would forever be termed "the birthplace of the atomic age."

The town of Los Alamos also introduced the state to massive federal funding for scientific purposes. Historian Chris Dietz has argued that the nearby Tewa-speaking pueblos of San Ildefonso, Santa Clara, and Cochiti used Los Alamos salaries to *preserve* their historic Native traditions. Pueblo leaders were able to purchase communal farm equipment, and numerous other Indians followed suit on an individual basis. It might not be too much to suggest that a legacy of big science (or, perhaps, big technology) also found its way into the colorful, if somewhat perplexing, art of the sophisticated hydraulic lifts that adorn the Española lowriders. . . .

The culture of science reached into other areas of the state as well. Historian Necah Stewart Furman has shown how the establishment of Sandia

National Laboratories in Albuquerque altered life in the Duke City. The rise of Kirtland Air Force Base, especially the closely related Special Weapons Laboratory, funneled even more federal monies into Bernalillo County. . . .

The name of Paddy Martínez is well known to all residents of Grants and Milan, for in the early 1950s the Navajo sheepherder discovered a chunk of uranium that inaugurated the biggest American mining boom since the California Gold Rush of 1849. Known previously as a spot to raise fine carrots, by the mid-1960s Grants basked in the reputation of the "Uranium Capital of the United States." By 1980 over 40 percent of the nation's uranium was mined and milled in the Grants Uranium Belt region, and the town reached a population of 11,500.

Robert Goddard chose Roswell to test his rocket experiments, but the hamlet of Alamogordo benefited even more from the demands of the war. Afterward, the Alamogordo Bombing Range (now White Sands Missile Range) commandeered an area larger than the state of Delaware. In 1976, Alamogordo dedicated an impressive Space Hall of Fame. It proudly called itself "Birthplace of Atomic Energy—Home of American Rocket Research."

The Very Large Array (VLA) radio telescope on the Plains of San Agustin, established in the mid-1970s, is the state's latest big science project. Here, amid grazing cattle and soaring falcons, astronomers maneuver six-story-high radio antennas to probe for the ultimate secrets of the universe. In 1989, the Cannon Air Force Base in Clovis was selected to house the nation's extensive F-III fighter-bomber fleet. Such massive federal expenditures have produced a genuine scientific subculture. On a per-capita basis, New Mexico has more scientific and technical workers than any other state. No area of New Mexico remains unaffected by this scientific world. Whatever the future holds, however, the last half century of the Culture of Big Science has forever altered the New Mexico landscape. The state could never return to a pre-science economy.

Third is the culture of tourism. If one excludes the federal and state payrolls, in 1992 tourism still ranked as the main source of income and employment for the state. Recent estimates put the dollar amounts at 2.2 billion; over fifty-three thousand New Mexicans are somehow involved with tourism.

Originally part of the highway department, from the late 1930s forward the state Tourist Bureau did its best to acquaint the nation with the wonders of New Mexico. All sections of the state joined in this fifty-year crusade of self-promotion, some more effectively than others. But three sectors have parlayed their tourist appeal into a genuine international following. These were the Gallup Indian Ceremonial, the celebration of New Mexico skiing, and "the selling of Santa Fe."

In the late 1930s, northern New Mexico boasted several small ski areas in Las Vegas, Taos, and Santa Fe. By the early 1970s, New Mexico's slopes had begun to attract skiers from all over the nation. Although the industry suffered setbacks in the 1980s, northern New Mexico still rivals Utah and Colorado for the best in intermountain American skiing.

The selling of Santa Fe, especially its world of crafts and fine arts, has become the most successful tourist tale of the postwar era. In 1990, Santa Fe had about 200 galleries. It also ranked third in the nation in art, trailing only New York City and Los Angeles. Significantly, it ranked first in the category of selling art to buyers outside of the region. . . . By 1980 Old Town in Albuquerque had twenty-four galleries; estimates put the Albuquerque art market at 12 million dollars a year. The culture of tourism also provided American Indian artists with an increasing opportunity to market their work. . . .

For the fourth point, I want to turn to a more traditional concept of culture: Education, *belles-lettres*, music, and religion. . . . In 1992, UNM had grown to a school with twenty-six thousand students, several branch campuses, and international reputations in such fields as anthropology, Latin American Studies, and American Western History. The engineering and science departments all worked closely with the state's federal laboratories. New Mexico State University grew proportionately, and the regional colleges, such as Eastern New Mexico in Portales and Western New Mexico in Silver City, continued to serve local needs. New Mexico Highlands in Las Vegas emerged as "the Hispanic University" and continued to send many of its graduates into the political world. . . .

The second area of "high culture" involved music. Although music played a major role in both traditional Indian and Spanish societies, prior to World War II few scholars had paid much attention to it. . . .

University of New Mexico music professor John Donald Robb almost single-handedly revived interest in the state's Hispanic musical traditions. Traveling throughout the state, Robb set up his recorder at New Mexico weddings, sheep camps, funerals and campfires. But the center of the state's postwar musical scene belonged to the "Miracle of the Desert": the Santa Fe Opera. The Opera has proven to be one of Santa Fe's major attractions. Opening night invariably turns into a gala occasion. . . .

Like the world of music, New Mexican post–World War II *belles-lettres* soon moved from the provincial to the international. . . .

The most popular historian of New Mexico was the multitalented Fray Angélico Chávez. A Franciscan priest who served several New Mexico parishes, Chávez probably reached the widest audience with his evocative *My Penitente Land* (1974), which compared New Mexico with central Spain in perceptive and graceful prose. . . .

The sophistication of literature grew in step with the sophistication of historical writing. In 1966, playwright Mark Medoff moved to Las Cruces to teach at New Mexico State. His *Children of a Lesser God* won numerous awards and became a popular film. During the sixties, however, the state's Native voice began to be heard in several genres. Acoma poet Simon Ortiz collected his poems in *From Sand Creek* (1981), while N. Scott Momaday, who grew up at Jemez Pueblo, won a Pulitzer Prize for *House Made of Dawn* (1968). Laguna writer Leslie Marmon Silko achieved international fame with her novel *Ceremony* (1977). In general these were not happy voices.

During the same period, a number of Spanish-American writers consciously began to inaugurate a revived Hispanic literature. No one represented this theme better than UNM English professor Rudolfo Anaya. Author of several studies of New Mexico Hispanic life, Anaya's *Bless Me Ultima* (1974) told of a young man's coming of age in a small Hispanic village. . . .

The multiplicity of views that one finds in the state's literature was even more prevalent in the story of religion in New Mexico. At the end of World War II, New Mexico's religious scene was dominated by a predominantly Hispanic Catholic congregation served by Irish or French priests; a variety of Native faiths, both mingled with, and separate from, this Catholicism; a deep-rooted German Jewish community; and most of the mainline Protestant groups, led by the Presbyterians. Fifty years later, New Mexico had become a "spiritual land" that attracted both conventional and unconventional groups in large numbers. . . .

Since the late 1960s, however, the northern part of New Mexico has attracted a number of very distinct religious groups. In the early 1970s, a Sikh community began in the Española Valley. A mosque, Dar-al-Islam, was also established near Abiquiu, lasting from the early to the late 1980s. A small but thriving Zen center exists in Santa Fe. The New Age movement has also found a permanent home in "The City Different." By the early 1990s New Mexico had become a "spiritual magnet." The state seemed to draw in seekers from every religious group imaginable. As a Sikh leader recently observed, "God lives everywhere, but his mailing address is New Mexico...."

No discussion of modern New Mexican culture would be complete without mention of artist Georgia O'Keeffe and author Tony Hillerman. Both have transcended the boundaries between "high" and "popular culture." And both are forever linked with the New Mexican landscape. Well before her death in Santa Fe in 1986, critics had dubbed her America's most original artist; the nation's greatest woman painter; perhaps "the greatest woman painter in the world...."

The rise of the post–World War II "cultures" of landscape, science, tourism, high culture, and popular culture have transformed modern New Mexico. In many and subtle ways, they have intersected with the famed "Heroic Triad" of the Indian, Hispanic, and Anglo-Pioneer worlds. Few would disagree that the charm and uniqueness of New Mexico may be traced to the interaction of its various cultures. (Pp. 159–96)

—Ferenc M. Szasz

The Population Changes

Anglos and Hispanics are the two largest groups in New Mexico today. In 1940 Hispanics were the majority. This changed after World War II. Hispanics then became a minority group. Most newcomers were Anglo. Anglos made up the largest group until 1990.

Today, no group is a majority. In 2000 Hispanics made up about 42 percent of New Mexicans. Combined with Indians, Blacks, and Asians, they total about 55 percent of the people. The remaining 45 percent are Anglos. Thus New Mexico is a "minority-majority" state. This means that no one group has a majority. We are all part of a "minority group" in New Mexico.

Many Peoples Enrich New Mexico

New Mexico is a unique land. It is a land that has benefited from many groups of people. And among the people who have helped shape the state are its Black citizens. Blacks appear early in New Mexico's history. Indeed, the first Blacks came as explorers and settlers. They entered New Mexico alongside Spaniards. Later, they came as cowboys. They came as soldiers and miners. They came as former slaves. They were men and women searching for a better way of life.

Some of the Blacks who came settled in New Mexico's cities. Albuquerque was one such city. The first sizable number of Blacks in Albuquerque came with the railroad. Few, however, stayed in Albuquerque in the late 1800s. The city had little industry. It had few job openings. In addition, competition from Hispanics and Indians limited opportunities for Blacks.

Some Blacks did, of course, stay in Albuquerque. Those who did soon built a community for their people. They had their own church. The Grant Chapel African Methodist Church was founded in 1882. They held jobs as small businessmen and barbers. They worked as porters, cooks, and railroad workers. In 1912, when New Mexico became a state, about 100 Blacks lived in Albuquerque. By 1920 the Black population had grown to about 300. Many of these people had moved to Albuquerque after World War I.

Other Blacks settled in New Mexico's rural areas. One such area lay east of the Rio Grande in Doña Ana County. There, Blacks settled on land that companies sold them under long-term contracts. The land was thought to be worthless.

The Black settlers made the land valuable. They washed alkali out of the soil. They introduced cotton to the Rio Grande Valley. In time, the Blacks in the valley paid off their land contracts. After World War I they built the small town of Vado. Standing southeast of Las Cruces and slightly east of Interstate 10, Vado has remained a Black community.

Like Blacks everywhere New Mexico's Blacks have faced discrimination. In 1907, for example, three Black students were excluded from Albuquerque High School's graduation. They received their diplomas in a separate ceremony. And in 1926 the Doña Ana County schools were segregated. A separate school was built for the children who lived in Vado.

Yet New Mexico's Black citizens have endured these injustices. They have worked to end discrimination. Today Blacks live in many different parts of the state. They work in all kinds of jobs. Blacks have enjoyed success in politics and their professional lives. By their presence and their culture, they add much to New Mexico. They made up almost 2 percent of the state's population in 2000.

New Mexico's other minorities have continued to enrich New Mexico. New Mexico has over 173,000 American Indian residents. They make up about 9.5 percent of the state's population. Most of them live on one of their reservations in New Mexico. They have a long history of living in New Mexico, since they are the original settlers in the state.

SELECTION FROM
Roadside New Mexico
A Guide to Historic Markers

The Jicarilla Apache trace their ancestry to cultural groups that migrated from Canada around A.D. 1300 to 1400. As these groups, known as the *Athabascan*, reached the Rocky Mountain region and other places in North America, they developed linguistic differences and separated into distinct tribes. Among these were the Navajo, who settled in the northwestern portion of the state and the Apache, who roamed vast portions of New Mexico, Colorado, Oklahoma, and Texas Panhandle. Separate branches of the Apache tribe arose, including the Chiricahua in southwestern New Mexico, Mescalero in south-central New Mexico, and one group in northeastern and eastern New Mexico. After the Spanish encountered the latter group in the seventeenth century they named the Indians *Jicarilla*. *Jicarilla* is a Spanish word meaning "little cup" and likely refers to baskets woven by the Apaches from reeds.

The Jicarilla Apache were primarily hunters and gatherers and frequently crossed the plains on buffalo hunts. Archaeological evidence shows that the Apache also built small farming villages south of present-day Cimarron. In 1723, Comanche warriors began a series of attacks against the tribe. By the middle of the eighteenth century these attacks, together with encroachments by the French and Spanish onto the plains, had driven the Apache over the Sangre de Cristo Mountains and into the Rio Grande Valley.

After the Southwest became part of the United States in the mid-nineteenth century the government created land set-aside to provide permanent homes for Indians. The Jicarilla were the last tribe in the state to receive their own reservation. Although the Apache had been previously settled elsewhere, an Executive Order issued by President Grover Cleveland on February 11, 1887, established the current Jicarilla Apache Reservation in north-central New Mexico. The town of Dulce became the headquarters for the Jicarilla Agency. A second Executive

Order issued on November 11, 1907, augmented the size of the reservation to almost twice its original allotment. The new land gained ran south from roughly around Tapicito Ridge to just below present-day US 550. More recently, the Jicarilla have acquired El Poso Ranch and Thesis Ranch, bringing the size of their reservation to more than 840,000 acres.

As part of the 1987 centennial celebrating the Executive Order that created their reservation, a caravan of some 130 Jicarilla Apaches driving wagons and pickup trucks left Cimarron for Dulce on May 26 in a symbolic reenactment of the journey of their ancestors to their present home. Led by Adolphus Caramillo, who rode a horse he named *Amtrak*, the caravan wound its way through the mountain resort areas of Eagle Nest, Angel Fire, Taos, Abiquiu, Tierra Amarilla, and Chama, arriving in Dulce on June 14 after covering some two hundred miles. Later, the tribe worked with the New Mexico State Highway Department to designate NM 537 between US 550 (formerly NM 44) and US 64 as the "Jicarilla Apache Reservation Centennial Highway." (Pp. 48–49)

—David Pike

Asians and South Pacific Islanders make up about 1 percent of New Mexico's people. They are often recently arrived immigrants, especially since the 1980s. In particular many fled wars in Southeast Asia to find peace and a new life. New Mexico has given them both.

Some people move to New Mexico because it is a sunbelt state. The sunbelt is a region that reaches across the country. It stretches from North Carolina to southern California. Many Americans have moved to the sunbelt in recent years. They came looking for a milder climate. Some came here to retire. Others moved their businesses here. New Mexico has thus received newcomers from the north. Its greatest growth as a sunbelt state was during the 1970s. Since 1970 the population of New Mexico has grown faster than that of almost all other states.

New Mexicans Face the Future

Today there are more New Mexicans than ever. As the state grows, there are still questions that must be addressed. One of these has been around for centuries. That is the issue of water. History has taught us that New

Mexico is a dry land. In the north, irrigation uses acequias, or special ditches. These date from centuries ago but are vital even today. The acequia brings water to crops but its survival is in question.

SELECTION FROM
Acequia Culture
Water, Land, and Community in the Southwest

In the years ahead, acequia associations likely will assert their powers of rule making, probably with greater frequency and growing sophistication. Resistance at the local level, one case at a time, however, will not guarantee protection of the acequia culture as a whole. More broad-based policy and water-law reforms will be needed if communities are to survive as traditional water users. If left to chance, the forces of the water markets will allocate water to the highest bidder in the short run, without regard for historic uses or long-term sustainability. . . .

The crafts industries of the state and the region thrive in large part due to the setting in which objects and other handmade goods are produced by local artisans. Without water, these villages literally would dry up, as would the arts and crafts industry vital to the economic-development goals of the state of New Mexico. Policymakers should be mindful that acequia communities are a low-cost, renewable resource. Severing water rights from farmland for development purposes, on the other hand, eventually will erode the resource base that the acequia communities depend on. Because the tourism industry needs the rural and quaint village landscapes to sustain the attractions and amenities that visitors seek, elimination of acequia communities runs counter to tourism goals of the state.

It is widely acknowledged that conventional approaches to economic development in the rural West, based on mineral extraction, industrial relocation, and capital-intensive tourism have met with dismal results. Jobs may be created, but the benefits are inequitably distributed; growth may or may not occur, but poverty and underdevelopment persist, and in the process, the community loses control of the resources it needs for long-term sustainable economic activity. Acequia-based agriculture, however, promotes cultural tourism while supporting social policy values of self-reliance, anti-poverty, and grassroots democracy at work. Contemporary principles of rural environmental planning confirm that local resources should form the basis for guiding economic development. Such growth is sustainable and consistent with resource-base capacities: the natural, human, and cultural elements of development serve as the building blocks of any local economy. Such development is integrated with local institutions and conserves existing cultural resources. . . .

These are difficult issues, but as concluded in a study of water-rights transfers in the western states by the National Research Council, New Mexico represents a compelling case for recognition of social and water-equity values:

> In the nineteenth century, Anglo property concepts were
> superimposed over the more communal traditions of the pueblos
> and Hispanic irrigation communities. Today New Mexico has
> a sophisticated water allocation system that basically treats water
> as a commodity to maximize the efficiency of use of the resource.
> But the clash of cultures makes northern New Mexico special;
> there are allocation tensions [here] that do not exist in other
> states. . . . If one wanted to make a case for protecting communities
> as entities, northern New Mexico would be the example to use.

Some precedents to justify public-policy actions exist. Numerous times, governments at federal, state, and local levels have intervened in market arenas to preserve other natural resources and historic treasures: national forests, wildlife-refuge preserves, wetlands and other animal sanctuaries, land-trust territories, state open-space parks and trails, river-corridor *bosques*, historic main streets, town plazas, and buildings. In a parallel effort, acequia villages and towns should challenge the state to accept the proposition that their communities perpetuate a unique rural character important to the region and the state economy as a whole. Acequia officials can argue that these rural enclaves are cultural resources as priceless as scenic or forested areas and should be protected from urban spillover effects, commercial exploitation, and the pressures of economic conversion as a unique and valued way of life.

At the federal level, acequia communities located within land-grant boundaries possibly could pursue claims to "federally reserved water rights" along with national parks, Indian reservations, and other federal reservations of land in the West. If this designation was achieved, acequia water rights priorities would be based no later than on the date the land grant was confirmed and the settlers allowed to take possession. . . .

More widely, covering a much greater number of communities, acequias with pre-1848 water rights could pursue federal protection of their communal and customary water rights under the Treaty of Guadalupe Hidalgo. Article VIII of this international treaty with Mexico guaranteed Mexicans who resided in the conquered territory the right to continue in residence and to retain their property rights: "property of every kind . . . shall be inviolably respected." Though the treaty did not specifically mention water rights, lawyers and historians agree that property rights protected under the treaty most certainly encompassed water rights. The Treaty of Guadalupe Hidalgo predates the New Mexico state constitution by more than sixty years and the water code by more than a half-century.

Without intervention by government, rapid change will hasten the decline of an already endangered regional culture. The vital diversity of the rural landscape is tied to the acequia. It needs to be preserved. (Pp. 189–93)

—José A. Rivera

The amount of water in the state is limited. Scientists are uncertain how much ground water is available to New Mexicans. And they point out that droughts will continue. All New Mexicans need to be concerned about saving water.

SELECTION FROM
Civics for New Mexicans

Dear Ninth Graders:

Did you know that every time you eat a breakfast of eggs, bacon, buttered toast and milk the water bill for the meal is 510 gallons? Or that in 1980 the average American used 2,000 gallons of water each day, compared to 1,200 gallons in 1950?

East of the Mississippi River, where yearly rainfall is as much as 40 to 60 inches a year, your fellow ninth graders probably don't even think twice about the availability of water for their everyday needs.

But water is something that ninth graders—and many others in New Mexico including United States Senators like myself—have to think about and do something about.

The western United States receives the least rainfall of any section of the country. New Mexico receives a mere 10 to 20 inches a year. As much as 35 inches falls in the high mountains, but as little as six inches falls in the arid basins. Specialists tell us that this could spell trouble for New Mexicans in the central and southern areas in the [twenty-first] century.

Demand is expected to outstrip supply. In the year 2020, New Mexico's population will have more than doubled, with 3 million people producing a demand for 3.3 million acre feet of water each year. (An acre foot is the volume of water required to cover one acre of land to a depth of one foot.) Only 3 million acre feet will be available from traditional sources.

Western states have long recognized the water problem. Three treaties and eight interstate compacts allocate the flow of water in New Mexico's principal rivers. Court cases regarding the distribution of water have gone all the way to the U.S. Supreme Court.

As a member of the Senate's Environment and Public Works Committee and the Energy and Natural Resources Committee, I have worked with New Mexican officials to find solutions to our water problems before we face a crisis.

I also have been urging adoption of a national water policy, including a more rational system of sharing costs of water projects among different levels of government in order to discourage unnecessary projects. Congress has had difficulty passing water legislation and is spending only one-fourth of what it used to on water projects. In the absence of a sound national policy, it now takes more than 25 years to actually begin construction of a water project from the time the project is first conceived.

In New Mexico, one problem that needs to be attacked is the depletion of the Ogallala Aquifer in the state's eastern section. An aquifer is a natural reservoir of ground water, like a giant sponge, that is filled primarily by rain or snowmelt. The Ogallala Aquifer is the largest in the nation and is an important source of water for New Mexico, Colorado, Kansas, Nebraska, Oklahoma and Texas.

These states served by the aquifer produce 38 percent of the nation's livestock and 15 percent of its wheat, corn, grain, sorghum and cotton. The area depends heavily on irrigation, but a tremendous increase in irrigated land over the past 30 years has placed a great strain on the aquifer. Less than 7 million acre feet of water were withdrawn in 1950; more than 21 million acre feet were withdrawn in 1980. Natural refilling of the aquifer is not keeping pace with the withdrawal of water.

Because New Mexico has vast amounts of brackish ground water and because 90 percent of the state's water is used for agriculture, the Water Resources Research Institute at New Mexico State University and the Roswell Desalinization Test Facility are studying ways to make better use of available water. With my support, the Water Resources Research Institute has received federal money.

The researchers are attempting to find more efficient ways to deliver water and to develop crops that are more salt tolerant and are able to grow with less water. Also, the researchers are experimenting with growing fish and algae in brackish ground water.

Water is no light subject to New Mexicans. Next time you eat a half-pound steak, remember that 2,600 gallons of water were used to produce it. Add an ear of corn to your meal and another 61 gallons were used. We all must work to conserve water—with an eye toward our futures. (Pp. 31–33)

Your friend, Pete Domenici
United States Senator

New Mexico's Economy Expands

Also important today are changes in the economy that came after World War II. By 1990 fewer than three percent of New Mexicans still made their living in farming and ranching. Today, most of the state's agricultural products come from two areas. One area is along the Lower Rio Grande Valley. The other is the eastern plains. Of all 33 counties, Doña Ana leads the state in farm production. Roosevelt, Curry, and Chaves counties also produce many cash crops. The state's leading agricultural products are cattle, sheep, dairy products, and wool. The state produces other items such as hay, chile peppers, onions, and corn. Farmers also grow pecans, cotton, wheat, and sorghum.

The Permian Basin extends across parts of Texas and New Mexico. Natural gas comes from both northwestern and southeastern New Mexico. In the 1990s the value of natural gas produced in New Mexico was greater than oil.

The future of the oil and gas industries is uncertain. When prices rise, output goes up. When prices fall, output drops. Also, no one knows how long New Mexico can produce oil or gas.

For a while the mining of uranium and potash employed thousands.

Paddy Martínez, a Navajo sheepherder, found uranium near the town of Grants in 1950. This set off a mining boom in the area. Uranium is the source of atomic energy. It is used in making nuclear weapons. It is also used in nuclear power plants. However, in the 1980s the demand for uranium fell. Today, almost all uranium mining in New Mexico has stopped.

Potash was found much earlier, in 1925, near Carlsbad. Potash is mainly used as fertilizer. In 1978 New Mexico supplied over half the nation's potash. Recently, though, potash mining has dropped because of low prices.

New Mexico has become a center for weapons and scientific research. Los Alamos National Laboratory today does energy research. Sandia National Laboratories in Albuquerque still conducts nuclear research. It has also worked on new and improved sources of energy. Technology has also become important in recent years. Major electronics firms have moved to New Mexico. They make and develop electronic equipment. Their importance to New Mexico's economy continues to grow.

White Sands Missile Range has remained an important site for weapons and spacecraft testing and development. These facilities have employed many thousands of New Mexicans. White Sands also shows how New Mexicans adapt. Mining and other economic activity did not bring hoped-for jobs. So local citizens began pushing for a way to benefit from the unique environment of White Sands.

SELECTION FROM
White Sands
A History of a National Monument

The need to preserve White Sands did not originate as a result of the public's environmental outcries. As has been the case with other areas within the National Park system, the demand for preserving the dunes resided with a small, vocal special interest group, namely the Alamogordo Chamber of Commerce. The lure of tourist dollars mainly motivated the chamber and its leading spokesman, Tom Charles. They promoted White Sands as a potential playground to state and federal officials. While mining ventures seemed to promise jobs and riches for the region, these expectations were never fulfilled. In short order the value of White Sands shifted from purely commercial exploitation to the possibility of developing a lucrative tourist industry. . . .

The shift in emphasis from mining to tourism suggests that local developers and residents continued to view White Sands as an economic asset. . . .

It was the preservation-oriented National Park Service that insisted on the maintenance of White Sands as a natural area. . . . The geologic composition of White Sands, as well as its aesthetic qualities, made it appropriate for designation as national monument status . . .

The relationship between the Interior and the Defense departments has proved a mixed blessing. On the one hand the military prevented the private and commercial exploitation and despoliation of the land surrounding the monument and its resources. On the other, the nature of Defense Department activities has continuously undermined the National Park Service's mandate for preserving the dune field and its flora and fauna. . . .

Annually White Sands National Monument ranks second only to Carlsbad Caverns National Park in attendance in the National Park Service's Southwest Region. White Sands National Monument's popularity as a recreational area contributes immeasurably to New Mexico's tourism industry and to the economies of the surrounding communities. . . .

White Sands offers many natural wonders: magnificent desert sunrises bursting over the crests of the Sacramento Mountains; striking fiery sunsets silhouetting the distant Organ and San Andres mountains; blinding gypsum windstorms; driving winter snowstorms; searing summer days and refreshingly cool evenings; spectacular thunder and lightning storms; sporadic and intense lifegiving desert rainstorms. . . . Equally memorable is a full moon excursion into the Heart of the Dunes—a night sky, crisp and clear, with a million stars, a full moon, and the wide expanse of rolling gypsum dunes. . . .

White Sands has become much more than just a site for picnics or a recreational playground; the dune field's fragile ecosystem and gypsum scenery have at last become important for their own sake. (Pp. 155–79)

—*Dietmar Schneider-Hector*

New Mexico has also been an energy-producing state. Its mineral wealth remains large. New Mexico will continue to produce energy. Atomic energy is part of both the future and the past in New Mexico. Throughout the world and in the United States, too, are found peaceful and safe uses of atomic energy. Electricity is produced from atomic sources. But some other atomic work leaves waste products that must be carefully dealt with since they are radioactive and therefore very dangerous. A special place near Carlsbad has been built to forever hold radioactive waste from weapons research.

SELECTION FROM

Nuclear Reactions
The Politics of Opening a Radioactive Waste Disposal Site

The Waste Isolation Pilot Plant (WIPP), beneath the flatlands of southeastern New Mexico outside Carlsbad, is the first facility of its kind in the world. It is the most elaborate landfill built to date to permanently house mankind's deadliest garbage. Open since 1999, the project is intended to entomb, in underground rock salt, four decades' worth of protective gloves, tools, cleaning rags, glassware, and other cast-off items that have been contaminated with radioactive materials used in building nuclear weapons. It cost around $2 billion to build and costs $200 million a year to operate; the final price tag for preparing, shipping, and disposing of waste there has been estimated to be as high as $29 billion. More than 6 million cubic feet of waste will be sent to the site—an amount equal to 850,000 55-gallon drums, enough to fill more than 65 rooms that are each about the size of a football field.

The underground area of WIPP where the waste is buried looks like no other mine. Situated more than 2,000 feet inside the earth and accessible by a five-minute elevator ride, it features a vast seven-mile network of manmade tunnels connecting the cavernous storage rooms. Measuring gauges and monitoring instruments line the floors, walls, and ceilings, which are flecked with gray and orange-pink salt crystals. The circulation of air within the facility is strictly controlled, but dust gets around; workers say that after enough time underground, they can taste the gritty salt for days afterward. . . .

The materials heading to WIPP travel by truck from more than a dozen federal bomb factories and research complexes. They include the former Rocky Flats plant near Denver, New Mexico's Los Alamos National Laboratory, Idaho National Engineering and Environmental Laboratory, Washington State's Hanford Nuclear Reservation, Tennessee's Oak Ridge National Laboratory, and South Carolina's Savannah River Plant. The wastes are often described as "low-level." That characterization is misleading. Instead they are "transuranic," meaning they contain elements heavier than uranium. Transuranic waste is neither high-level nor low-level, although it shares characteristics of both. The main transuranic element in WIPP's waste is plutonium, a man-made element used in making the "trigger" that sets off a nuclear warhead. Plutonium's alpha particles travel only inches and cannot penetrate skin or even a sheet of paper. Workers can actually handle most waste drums by hand, as long as they remain sealed. But if it is inhaled, swallowed, or absorbed into the bloodstream through a cut, an amount of plutonium as small as one-millionth of a gram can cause cancer. Plutonium not only is dangerous but long-lived—it takes 24,360 years to lose half of its radioactivity.

The theory behind WIPP is that after the wastes are put 2,150 feet underground, the rock salt will naturally collapse around them, forming a tight cocoon that seals them off and prevents their escape. Salt has been shown to move rapidly to heal fissures and close openings, and it is expected that less than a century after the final waste drum is buried, the materials will be completely encapsulated. Aboveground, meanwhile, large and elaborately designed markers will serve as futuristic "no trespassing" warnings. They will contain a variety of symbols in languages other than English, since there is no guarantee that modern words will outlive the dangerousness of the waste. The expectation is that no one will drill or dig into the site and allow radioactivity to escape and that no natural geological occurrences will allow the materials to reach groundwater supplies or nearby rivers. . . .

The New Mexico project has been one of the most tangled energy policy quagmires of recent decades. Before the initial waste shipment in March 1999, it had been actively planned for a quarter of a century, and in essence built for years. But it was plagued by more than a decade of delays and has remained controversial since its opening. The problems and fights that led to those delays and fueled those controversies have widened the gulf between America's ability to create sophisticated weapons and its ability to successfully show it can clean up after them. . . .

The biggest challenge in storing nuclear waste has been overcoming public resistance. . . . With WIPP, environmentalists and other critics have vociferously argued that the plant is an ill-advised attempt to address waste storage. . . .

Critics argue that the plant will not "solve" the government's nuclear waste storage problem because it remains relatively small in scope. It is slated to dispose of less than one-quarter of the wastes generated from weapons manufacturing. (Pp. 1–6)

—*Chuck McCutcheon*

CHAPTER TEN

Modern Artists and Writers

SELECTION FROM
New Mexico's History
A Message for the Future

Norman Petty needs a statue. Born and educated in Clovis, New Mexico where he directed his school's band, he would go on to make history. Still, Petty is unsung when compared to the many better-known people that he helped to achieve fame.

Petty was born in 1927 and died in 1984. He spent his whole life in and around his hometown. He loved music and by the 1950s was a professional musician. He liked popular, rock 'n' roll and named his first group "The Torchy Swingsters." He was good enough in his youth to score the famous Duke Ellington song "Mood Indigo."

In 1954, Petty decided to create music in a different way. Rather than be up front playing it he decided to work behind the scenes creating it. He purchased his uncle's vacant store that was located next to his parents' filling station. There he built and installed a state-of-the-art recording studio. Within two years he would make rock 'n' roll history.

Petty did more than record. He arranged and produced. He clearly became a major influence on his industry and nothing could be more illustrative than his relationship with Buddy Holly.

Holly traveled to Petty's studio after a bad experience trying to record in Nashville. After three sessions in Tennessee he was judged "the biggest no talent I ever worked with." Yet, with Petty, Buddy Holly became a national household name.

On their first night working together they recorded two songs, "I'm Looking for Someone to Love" and "That'll Be the Day." In the next fifteen months Holly and his band, the Crickets, recorded sixteen more rock 'n' roll classics. In the process, they created the "Clovis sound." John Lennon later claimed that the Beatles' first forty songs consciously tried to recreate the Clovis sound as they mimicked Buddy Holly. The Rolling Stones' first hit single was a cover of Holly's "Rave On." Paul McCartney, Lennon's longtime partner, eventually purchased the publishing rights to all of Holly's songs.

Norman Petty, who was the genius behind Holly, launched many careers in Clovis. Petty influenced Roy Orbison, Waylon Jennings, and a lesser known group from Raton, New Mexico called the Fireballs. The Fireballs are known for their still popular song "Sugar Shack" that they recorded with Petty. Petty's own group, the Roses, that he used in the studio has been inducted into the Hall of Fame in Nashville.

Norman Petty clearly influenced rock 'n' roll. He was a forceful man who did not hesitate to make a suggestion. Nevertheless, he recognized and allowed talent to express its respective genius. He encouraged experimentation. He intentionally created a "hot house" environment to nourish and produce the result of the collective energy of those involved with the sessions. An example of this is having the drummer playing an empty box that sat on his knees. This technique was used in Holly's songs, "Not Fade Away" and "Everyday." Petty suggested the use of a miniature xylophone in Holly's "Everyday."

Today, Lubbock, Texas, just across the border from Clovis, honors its native son Buddy Holly with a prominent statue. Such an honor for the man who made Holly is long overdue in New Mexico. (forthcoming)

—*Thomas Chávez*

New Mexico Is Home to Famous Painters

New Mexico has become a haven for gifted artists. Today, as in the past, these artists have drawn inspiration from their surroundings. Some have had lengthy careers. Their talent has provided a link between past and present.

Many regard Georgia O'Keeffe as New Mexico's most famous painter. Like others, she fell in love with the landscape. She began visiting and painting the land in the 1920s. She finally settled at Abiquiu after World War II. O'Keeffe continued her brilliant career until her death in 1986 at the age of 98.

Peter Hurd also gained fame as a painter. Born in Roswell, Hurd lived and worked at his ranch at San Patricio. There he painted the land and people of southern New Mexico. His career lasted until his death in 1984. One of his favorite subjects was the Hondo Valley.

New Mexico's Indian painters have gained fame as well. One of these is Pablita Velarde. A Santa Clara artist, Velarde is best known for her paintings and murals in public buildings. In addition, her paintings hang in museums across the nation. Velarde's daughter, Helen Hardin, became a famous painter in her own right.

SELECTION FROM

A Woman's Place
Women Writing New Mexico

Pablita Velarde accomplished success in her professional career with the help of Margarete and Fred Chase from the Enchanted Mesa Gallery in Albuquerque. In 1956, Enchanted Mesa had begun to exhibit all of Velarde's work, and the sales of her paintings eventually increased. Meanwhile, she was getting back in touch with Santa Clara. She started visiting the Pueblo to listen to her father retell the stories she had heard from him as a young girl. She has explained her motives for recording these stories as an evolving awareness of the need for someone to get them down on paper. Initially, she just wanted to preserve the stories for her children, who had a hard time learning them outside of the Pueblo. "My kids used to laugh at me when I was trying to tell them the story," Velarde explained in an interview. "They couldn't picture it in their heads . . . so I painted the picture first and then I read them the story the way I had written it—and then they understood. . . . Before they saw the picture, they didn't even know what you were talking about."

One of the pictures Velarde initially painted for her children, *Old Father Story Teller*, won immediate critical recognition, including the grand prize at the 1955 Inter-Tribal Ceremonial in Gallup. This painting's success led her to consider publishing her stories, complete with illustrations, for a larger audience. "I decided to write all those old stories into a book," she has said, "so that every Indian child and children of every race could forever have these Indian stories."

Renewed contact with a former supporter further encouraged her in this project. During a 1956 Christmas vacation with her children, Velarde got a flat tire in Globe, Arizona, and called the only person she knew in town: Dale Stuart King, the man who had commissioned her for the murals at Bandelier. Retired from the Park Service, King was now interested in publishing books and had started a small regional press. When he heard about Velarde's manuscript idea, he offered to publish it. Velarde completed *Old Father Story Teller*, which consisted of six stories accompanied by painted illustrations. It was published in 1960. According to historian Sally Hyer, Velarde thus became the first Pueblo woman to publish a book. A regional audience eager for American Indian art and stories received the book warmly. One association of printers and booksellers, the Rounce and Coffin Club of Los Angeles, selected the book for its annual Western Books exhibit.

But some residents of the Pueblo did not approve of Velarde's publication of the stories and traditions of Santa Clara. Even her father, whose stories formed the heart of the book, had expressed reservations about the project. "My father helped me reluctantly because he believed that telling a story was better than writing it," Velarde has explained. In addition to his caution about disclosing sacred stories, he feared writing them would diminish their power to live on—after all, they had lasted for generations through oral storytelling alone. Eventually, in her words, she "convinced him that this was the only way to preserve our culture. After that he became interested and often sent for me to come back to Santa Clara to hear more stories." Even then, Velarde described, he might ask her to wait with him in silence before he spoke:

> Sometimes we would sit there for hours, perhaps all day, not saying anything, for that was the way the Indians were. It was a way of being respectful to the Ancient Ones, to the past and to the gods. Time meant nothing. When I would get impatient for him to talk, he would say: "You talk too much. The fruit tree has too much fruit. The tree limbs break and fall to the ground. Be still and listen to what is inside you." Other times he would be moved to talk. The fruit tree would be bowed down with fruit, and I would take home many of Old Father's stories.

Velarde eventually decided to leave out some of what she and her father discussed, because of his wishes and out of respect for the Santa Clara community.

Her father was, in the end, pleased with the project. Velarde described his reaction to seeing the published book as a happy moment for both him and her: "I could tell by his expression that he was connecting the story with the pictures. . . . I knew he was getting kind of a thrill out of knowing that he had something to do with a book. And when he finished, he said, 'Isn't it nice that we did it?' He put 'we' in there!" Through the creation of the book, Velarde was able both to renew her relationship with her father and to provide what she saw as a service to Santa Clara, preservation of its old stories.

The book features six such stories, all told to a group of children by a character named Old Father. On special occasions, such as the Buffalo and Deer Dance, or on long winter nights, Old Father shares his stories with these listeners. "The Stars," "Sad Eyes," and "First Twins" explain fundamental beliefs of Santa Clara culture: they tell, respectively, how the people arrived in Santa Clara, how the deer dance ceremonial started, and how the first Koshares (Pueblo intermediaries between everyday life and supernatural life) came to be. The other three stories, "Enchanted Hunter," "Turkey Girl," and "Butterfly Boy," teach lessons through recounting individual events.

Velarde's children and grandchildren formed the original intended audience for the stories, but publication meant that other children, and adults, read them as well. At moments in the text, this intended larger audience clearly seems to be a non-Indian one. When the narrator lists the constellations by their Tewa names but with European names following in parentheses, or when she steps back from Old Father's story to explain basic elements of Santa Clara ceremonials such as the Koshares, she addresses readers who may have never been to Santa Clara or any of the Pueblos. (Pp. 251–55)

—Maureen Reed

So, too, did R. C. Gorman find Indian and non-Indian audiences. Born on the Navajo reservation, Gorman became a painter like his father, Carl. (Carl Gorman was also a Navajo Code Talker during World War II; see pp. 78–82.) The younger Gorman settled in Taos. His paintings hang in art galleries and in private homes around the world.

SELECTION FROM
Carl Gorman's World

After leaving Ganado Mission High School, R. C. [Gorman] had spent four years in the navy, studying at the Guam Territorial College from 1951 to 1955. Then he attended Arizona State College in 1955 (now Northern Arizona University) in Flagstaff and entered Mexico City College in 1958 (later called the University of the Americas) on a Navajo Tribal scholarship. Then he returned for further studies at the San Francisco State College. By the early 1960s he had had one-man shows in the Bay Area of San Francisco. His work often bordered on the abstract, but still retained a strong "Indian" feeling. "The reservation is my source of inspiration for what I paint," R. C. said, "but I never realized this until I found myself in some far-flung place like the tip of Yucatan. Perhaps when I stay on the reservation I take too much of what it has to offer for granted. While there, I paint very little. Off the reservation, it is my realization of reality." (Pp. 81–82)

—Henry Greenberg and Georgia Greenberg

New Mexico Is Home to Famous Writers

Other New Mexico artists have in recent years won fame as writers. One of these was Erna Fergusson. One of her earliest works was *Dancing Gods*. It detailed New Mexico and Arizona Indian ceremonials. When she died in 1964, she was regarded as the first lady of New Mexico letters.

Another writer, Paul Horgan, grew up in Albuquerque. He later moved to Roswell and then out of state. Horgan included New Mexico themes in many of his books. He won the Pulitzer Prize in 1955 for his *Great River*. This book tells the history of the people who have lived along the Rio Grande. In 1976 Horgan won a second Pulitzer Prize for his *Lamy of Santa Fe*. It tells the story of Santa Fe's first bishop.

John Nichols has lived in Taos, New Mexico, since 1969. He is the author of many novels and screenplays. Three of his novels depict life in New Mexico's northern mountain communities. *The Milagro Beanfield War* is the first and best known of the three. Novelist Tony Hillerman has also gained fame. He is today recognized as one of the nation's best mystery writers. His novels are mainly set on Navajo land. Hillerman describes in detail Navajo beliefs and customs.

SELECTION FROM
Talking Mysteries
A Conversation With Tony Hillerman

Funny how you never rid yourself of the psychological baggage you collect as a child. At about nine, I became aware that two kinds people make up the world. Them and us—the town boys and the country boys. . . .

I have since become old enough to know the above is mostly nonsense. Konawa, Oklahoma (home of the town boys), with its main street, two banks, drugstore, ice house, theatre where a movie was shown every Saturday, and competitive pool halls, wasn't much more urbane than Sacred Heart, Oklahoma, the crossroads with a filling station and cotton gin, which was the center of our country-boy universe. But wisdom about such things doesn't change ingrained attitudes. When I met the Navajos I now so often write about, I recognized kindred spirits. Country boys. More of us. Folks among whom I felt at ease. When I saw them standing around the fringes of a Zuni Shalako ceremonial, dressed in their "going-to-town" velvet and silver but still looking ill at ease, bashful, and very much impressed by the power of the town-boy neighbors, I saw myself, and my kinfolks, and my country friends. That begins explaining why I use a Navajo Tribal Policeman as my Sherlock Holmes, and The People who herd their sheep in the mountains and deserts of the Navajo Reservation as the background of my mystery novels. It is part of the reason I use the culture of The People as the turning point of my plots. But there's more to it than that.

The first Navajos I saw happened to be engaged in an Enemy Way, one of the curing ceremonials The People conduct to bring themselves back into harmony with their universe. It was July 1945. I was just back from Word War II, a very senior private first class with a patch over a damaged eye and a cane to help a gimpy leg. I had a sixty-day convalescent furlough and I found a job (in August 1945, anyone alive could find a job) driving a truckload of pipe from Oklahoma City to an oil well drilling site north of Crownpoint on the Navajo "checkerboard" Reservation. Suddenly, a party of about twenty Navajo horsemen (and women) emerged from the piñons and crossed the dirt road in front of me. They were wearing ceremonial regalia and the man in front was carrying something tied to a coup stick. These were a far cry from the cotton-chopping, baseball-playing Pottawatomies and Seminoles from my past. I was fascinated. Forty years later, I am still fascinated.

What I had seen was the "stick carrier's" camp of an Enemy Way ceremonial making its ritual delivery of the "scalp" to the camp of the patient. He turned out to be a just-returned serviceman like myself—who was being restored to beauty with his people and cured of the disharmony of exposure to foreign cultures. As it happened, it was the same phase of the same ceremony that I would use to make the plot hold together in my first mystery. But twenty years would pass before that would happen. (Pp. 24–26)

— Tony Hillerman and Ernie Bulow

Mark Medoff came to Las Cruces in 1966. A teacher at New Mexico State University, Medoff wrote *Children of a Lesser God.* This play won a Tony Award. Tonys are awarded for outstanding Broadway productions. The main female character in Medoff's award-winning play is deaf. The play's theme is communication between people who can and cannot hear.

Hispanic and Indian Writers Are Important

In recent years Hispanic and Indian writers have also gained fame. Rudolfo Anaya has used his love and knowledge of Hispanic culture to write novels, plays, and screenplays. Born in Pastura, his most famous works are *Bless Me, Ultima* and *Heart of Aztlán.* Both are set in and around Guadalupe County. Before Anaya's books were written, though, other Hispanic writers told about the New Mexico they knew and loved.

SELECTION FROM
Tradiciones Nuevomexicanas
Hispano Arts and Culture of New Mexico

Literature in the Middle and Late Twentieth Century
Benjamín Read, a nineteenth-century journalist, published Spanish-language newspapers. He also began the trend of publishing in English. It was a trend

that grew as the twentieth century advanced. Another prominent legislator, Adelina (Nina) Otero-Warren, wrote her nostalgic autobiography (*Old Spain in Our Southwest*, 1936) in English, as did Cleofas Jaramillo (*The Genuine New Mexico Tasty Recipes*, 1939; *Shadows of the Past*, 1941; *Romance of a Little Village Girl*, 1955), Fabiola Cabeza de Baca Gilbert (*The Good Life, New Mexico Traditions and Food*, 1949; *We Fed Them Cactus*, 1954), and Aurora Lucero-White Lea (*Literary Folklore of the Hispanic Southwest*, 1953). These women sought to examine New Mexico's past and to preserve the traditional folkways before they passed into obscurity. This they did in fiction, folklore, and auto-biographies, including a culinary autobiography combining recipes with mem-oirs. Miguel A. Otero—a governor of New Mexico—wrote a three-volume autobiography entitled *My Life on the Frontier* (1935).

A common literary theme during this period seems to be a looking back to the old life—or as someone once described this process, "walking into the twentieth century backwards." *Nuevomexicano* writers drew their inspiration from oral tradition, pre-Territorial days, and earlier writers. In a survey of Hispanic literature nationwide, one writer describes New Mexico as the one state where contemporary writers are strongly tied to the region's tradition and history.

The decade of the 1960s saw a revival of *Nuevomexicano* literary activity. The difference was that the Chicano literary movement flourished nation-wide, essentially jump-started by the Civil Rights Movement and the politi-cal climate of the 1960s, which was more open to formerly marginalized cultures, even if only by force. Further, the increase in availability of higher education and opportunities for national and international travel opened the world to *Nuevomexicano* writers who then interacted with kindred spirits in other areas of the nation and at gatherings and conferences focusing on the various civil rights issues. As if on cue, publishers were ready to consider the works of emerging writers, even as universities were ready to train and pro-vide a forum for their ideas.

Chicano literature, as it was now called, helped fan the flames of the farm-worker movement, and helped writers grapple with political, economic, and educational concerns, as well as concerns over the passage of cultural mores from one generation to the next. Not surprisingly, many of the first writers of this period were those who could tap into the oral tradition.

In the 1970s and 1980s, a new generation of *Nuevomexicanos* found con-tinued opportunities to travel, study, reflect, write, and publish, particularly women. The emergence of Hispanic-run publishers like Arte Público Press and El Grito was mirrored in New Mexico by the emergence of El Norte Publications and *Blue Mesa Review*. In the 1990s, Ana Pacheco founded *La Herencia del Norte*, a quarterly magazine offering reminiscences, biographies, poetry, recipes, cultural studies, and herbal advice from established and emerging writers statewide.

Numerous creative writers and poets have emerged in the second half of the twentieth century. Here is a very brief sampling.

Sabine Ulibarrí (1919–2003)

His stories celebrate the pastoral life of old New Mexico. This short-story writer, poet, and essayist was born in Tierra Amarilla in the heart of northern New Mexico, and raised on a ranch by college-educated parents. In World War II, he flew thirty-five missions as an Air Force gunner; after the war he entered college. He earned a doctorate in Spanish and ultimately taught at every level from primary school to being a professor at the University of New Mexico. . . .

The short stories are populated with cowboys, sheriffs, folk healers, *hermanos*, and plain village folk. He has received numerous awards, including the White House Hispanic Heritage Award in 1989. He has published two books of poems, *Al cielo se sube a pie* (*You Reach Heaven on Foot*, 1966), and *Amor y Ecuador* (*Love and Ecuador*, 1966). His short-story collections include *Tierra Amarillo* (1971), *Mi abuela fumaba puros y otros cuentos de Tierra Amarilla* (*My Grandmother Smoked Cigars and Other Stories of Tierra Amarilla*, 1977), *Primeros encuentros/First Encounters* (1982), and others.

Rudolfo Anaya (b. 1937)

Born in Pastura, New Mexico, Anaya earned degrees in English, and Guidance and Counseling at the University of New Mexico in the 1960s and early 1970s. He directed the creative writing program at the University of New Mexico until his retirement. He has received numerous national and international awards for his works. His first novel, *Bless Me, Ultima* (1971), tells the story of a boy's coming of age in rural New Mexico, and is partly autobiographical. It represents a search for identity between *Nuevomexicano* and Pueblo cultures, and carries many references to Indian, Spanish, and Asian cultures. *Bless Me, Ultima* has touched more lives worldwide than any other work of Chicano literature, with one million copies in print in English, Spanish, French, Italian, Russian, and Japanese.

Other works include *Heart of Aztlán* (1976), *Tortuga* (1979), *The Silence of the Llano* (1982), *Alburquerque* (1992), *Zia Summer* (1996) and many more. He has also written plays, poetry, and children's stories, including *The Farolitos of Christmas*. His *Aztlán: Essays on the Chicano Homeland* was co-edited with Francisco Lomelí. Ever supportive of emerging *Nuevomexicano* writers, he has co-edited anthologies, including *Cuentos Chicanos* (1980) and *Voces/Voices* (1987), and together with his wife Patricia, established the Premio Aztlán literary prize given annually in New Mexico. Anaya's works often recall the idea of *Aztlán*, the mythical origin of the Aztec culture, thought to comprise what is now the five Southwestern states. The Chicano literary movement derived much inspiration from the idea of *Aztlán* as a source of imagery, symbols, and myths. Another theme in Anaya's works is the reestablishment of harmony and social order by drawing from traditional folkways.

Denise Chávez (b. 1948)

Ms. Chávez holds a degree in creative writing and has taught at the University of Houston and currently teaches at New Mexico State University in Las Cruces. Her work was chosen for inclusion in the *Norton Anthology of American Literature* and *Mexican American Literature*, published by Harcourt Brace Jovanovich, representing an endorsement by the Anglo literary establishment.

Her writings include *The Last of the Menu Girls* (1986) and *Face of an Angel* (1993). In the latter, the author explores the limits of the written page. She uses two separate yet similar stories printed in two adjacent columns in one segment of the novel. *Face of an Angel* focuses on the life of a waitress and her various adventures with men. It is a bawdy, irreverent, and humorous examination of the feminist movement told through the life of a waitress who keeps making the wrong choices. The novel also includes several other unique Southwestern characters, both humorous and tragic.

She organizes the annual Border Book Festival held in Las Cruces to encourage Chicano literature. She is also an accomplished actor and playwright.

Pat Mora (b. 1942)

A poet and El Paso native with several published collections, Ms. Mora has published *Chants* (1984), *Borders* (1986), *Communion* (1991), *Nepantla: Essays from the Land in the Middle* (1993), and *Aunt Carmen's Book of Practical Saints* (1997). Mora's works draw their inspiration from the desert landscape and

Indian cultures. In *Communion*, her perspective is global as she explores ties with other women of the world; in *Borders* she explores the different kinds of borders humanity has devised, such as the one between El Paso and Las Cruces. She is included in this list because El Paso historically is part of New Mexico. Mora also has received national attention and awards, including inclusion in the Norton and Harcourt Brace Jovanovich textbooks.

Estevan Arellano (b. 1940)

A farmer, cultural activist, journalist, and photographer, Arellano is renowned in literary circles for his novel, *Inocencio: ni pica, ni escarda, pero siempre come el mejor elote* (*Inocencio: He Never Digs Nor Hoes, But Always Eats the Best Ears of Corn*). The only novel written in New Mexican Spanish, *Inocencio* won the prestigious José Fuentes Mares Literary Prize in Mexico in 1991. In the 1970s, Arellano was active in the *Academia de la Nueva Raza* in Embudo, New Mexico, which conducted pioneer oral history projects and published a journal and a folklore collection.

Jimmy Santiago Baca (b. 1952?)

Baca's childhood and youth have colored his life and works for many years. He was abandoned as a child (hence the uncertain birthdate) and grew up in Albuquerque's South Valley. He began writing in prison. Those works were not about being Chicano, but about being in prison, and were published in *Immigrants in Our Own Land* (1979). Other works include *Working in the Dark: Reflections of a Poet of the Barrio* (1992), *Black Mesa Poems* (1989), *Martín*, and *Meditations on the South Valley* (1987). *Martín* is his autobiographical epic poem.

Martín, like many of his works, is strongly influenced by the past, but more out of pain and profound sadness than longing and nostalgia. His work is full of contrasts. His *mestizo* heritage comes alive in his poetry, and yet the reader also glimpses life in the Heights of Albuquerque (that is, Anglo life). In *Martín*, he reviews his life and determines not to repeat the mistakes of his parents. He also seeks salvation from the spirits of his ancestors. (Pp. 311–14)

—*Mary Montaño*

Famous Indian writers also have New Mexico roots. Although a Kiowa Indian, N. Scott Momaday grew up at Jemez Pueblo. His novel *House Made of Dawn* won the Pulitzer Prize in 1969. This novel draws upon the writer's early years in New Mexico.

The Nature of Native American Poetry

N. Scott Momaday has been cited as an inspiration by more contemporary Indian writers than any other author. *House Made of Dawn* and his autobiographical book of Kiowa legend and history, *The Way to Rainy Mountain*, provided a model for authors such as Dakota poet and fiction writer, Elizabeth Cook-Lynn. Momaday established the basis for contemporary Indian writing through his observations about the power and proper use of language and the reciprocal human relationship to place. While these, his best-known works, are prose, both contain poetry, which is Momaday's first love as a writer. Momaday is profoundly influenced by the oral literatures of the Kiowa, Navajo, and Pueblo cultures. His appropriation of the oral tradition to personal experience is key to understanding Momaday's poetry.

Born February 27, 1934, at Lawton, Oklahoma, Momaday was given the Kiowa name Tsoai-talee (Rock-tree Boy) during the first summer of his life by Phd-lohk, a Kiowa elder. His Kiowa father, Al Momaday, and his mother, Natachee Scott Momaday, of Cherokee, Scottish, and French descent, took him to *Tsoai* (the Kiowa name for Devil's Tower) in Wyoming when he was six months old, further bonding his identity to that place. His parents raised him on the Navajo Reservation at Shiprock, New Mexico, and Chinle and Tuba City, Arizona, and at Jemez Pueblo in New Mexico, where they had administrative and teaching jobs. Both influenced their son's writing—Al, with his paintings and his stories from the Kiowa oral tradition; Natachee, with her love of reading and writing literature. Momaday attended junior high and high school in Santa Fe, Albuquerque, and Bernalillo, then left the region in 1951 to complete high school at a military academy in Fort Defiance, Virginia. He returned to Albuquerque and completed a B.A. in political science at the University of New Mexico in 1958. Momaday then began teaching on the Jicarilla Apache Reservation at Dulce, New Mexico. Momaday received a Wallace Stegner Creative Writing Fellowship at Stanford University in 1959 and moved to California. There he completed a Ph.D. in 1963. He has taught at the University of California, Santa Barbara and Berkeley, Stanford

University, the University of Moscow, the University of New Mexico, the University of Regensburg in Germany, and the University of Arizona, where he has been Regents Professor of English since 1981. (Pp. 31–32)

—Norma C. Wilson

Leslie Marmon Silko of Laguna has also written several novels. A major theme in her books is the struggle to preserve Pueblo culture in the modern world.

SELECTION FROM

Leslie Marmon Silko
A Collection of Critical Essays

The publication of her widely praised first novel *Ceremony* in 1977 established Leslie Marmon Silko as a notable new talent in contemporary literature. Modifying the traditional novel to reflect her Indian culture, Silko experiments with a form that would continue to characterize her writing. The long-awaited *Almanac of the Dead* (1991) exhibited new facets of her extraordinary talent. This second novel is more complex than *Ceremony*—in fact, more so than any other novel of the latter part of the century. Poised between these two texts, the collection of short fiction, photographs, and autobiography entitled *Storyteller* (1981) confirmed Silko's determination to alter literary forms to accommodate her own heritage. (P. i)

—Louise K. Barnett

New Mexico Is Home to Gifted Craftspeople

The list of painters and writers goes on. So, too, does the list of other artists. Patrocinio Barela and George López gained recognition as modern santeros. Barela's santos first caught the public eye during the 1930s. George López began crafting santos more recently. He carried on the tradition of López family woodcarvers in Cordova. Also, craftspeople still weave fine blankets at Chimayó.

SELECTION FROM

Nuevomexicano Cultural Legacy
Forms, Agencies, and Discourse

In the mid-1980s, 137 Hispanic weavers were identified as living in two northern New Mexico counties. This number has grown substantially in the past decade. Although these weavers, and those living in other areas of the state, are carrying on a centuries-old tradition, no two weave exactly alike nor do they have the same experiences to relate regarding their weaving. In an effort to present an introduction to contemporary Hispanic weavers and their lives, the Ortega family is discussed here. This family has been singled out because it reflects different facets of Hispanic weaving: commerce, innovation, and tradition....

The best-known family of weavers in northern New Mexico is the Ortega family of Chimayó. Billboards along the main highway between Santa Fe and Taos divert visitors through the countryside to this village where the family business is located. Tour buses regularly stop at the Ortegas' on their northbound and southbound routes.

Nicasio and Virginia Ortega originally established their business as a general store in 1918. Since then, it has gone through many remodelings, and visitors today find a large store geared to tourists' needs. Ortega's weavers produce a full range of woven items. The majority come in standardized sizes ranging from 4" x 4" coffee mug mats to the ever-popular 10" x 10" mats, long table runners (*congitas*), and twin or full-size bed blankets (*frazadas*). Rugs and cushions also come in standardized sizes. Various items of clothing such as vests, coats, ponchos, and purses are made from loom-woven fabric and are displayed on many racks and shelves....

The Ortegas' longevity in Chimayó and their prominence as weavers have made them a part of northern New Mexico's elite. A main irrigation *acequia* was named after the Ortegas, and the family maintains its own nineteenth-century chapel, the Oratorio de San Buenaventura, in the old Plaza del Cerro. During the past half-century, David Ortega has been active in politics, has promoted the revival of Spanish colonial arts, and has been instrumental in bringing paved roads, a fire department, and a dump site to the village of Chimayó.

The Ortegas' success lies not only in the family's historical connection to the area, however, but also in the way in which they have developed their business. They draw on business practices outside of northern New Mexico. In the 1930s, when Anglo commercial weaving ventures opened in Santa Fe and sought Hispanic weavers to operate looms, David went to work for Burro Weavers. This experience afforded David a window on then-modern Anglo business practices. . . .

As Santa Fe and Taos gained prominence as art centers, the Ortegas capitalized on their High Road location linking the two cities and expanded their marketing efforts in the arts. In 1983, David's son, Andrew, and his wife, Evita, opened the Galeria Plaza del Cerro, now called the Galeria Ortega. At the gallery, the couple exhibits and sells the work of Hispanic, Indian, and Anglo artists and artisans of the area. More than any other weaving family in New Mexico, the Ortegas have received widespread newspaper and magazine publicity. On May 9, 1953, *The Saturday Evening Post* published an article by Neil M. Clark, "The Weavers of Chimayó: An Ancient New Mexico Craft Lives On." Other notable articles have appeared in *The New York Times*, *National Geographic*, *Vista Magazine*, *Countryside*, *Southwest Profile*, *Culture and Leisure*, and *New Mexico Magazine*. Many television, film, and video programs also have been devoted to the Ortegas.

The relatively small size of Ortega's Weaving Shop belies the scope of this large enterprise. Behind the scenes are dozens of weavers who weave in their own homes in a cottage industry. According to David, in 1983 the Ortegas had 115 looms and sixty active weavers whom they paid about a quarter of a million dollars in wages. The number of weavers has remained relatively constant. A decade later, Robert's roster of contract weavers still numbered sixty, but many more were working full time, indicating a greater commitment to the weaving profession. The weavers are located within a wide geographic radius. Most live in northern New Mexico, but some are scattered throughout the state; one weaver resided in El Paso, Texas.

Outside the community, David Ortega has been involved with the support of Hispanic arts and crafts. He has been a member of the board of the Spanish Colonial Arts Society and has served as a judge at Santa Fe's annual Spanish Market. David believes strongly in the role of Hispanic weaving as a vehicle for transmitting information about Hispanic culture. He regales visitors with stories regarding weaving while inserting his views about cultural values, historical incidents, and political preferences. David has helped fill the notebooks of dozens of researchers and journalists seeking information about

Chimayó and Hispanic weaving, opening family records and photo archives and proudly displaying family heirloom weavings.

Mr. Ortega has been a successful entrepreneur who has earned the respect of his community. His sensitivity to his market, his ability to recruit and retain weavers, his participation in the greater business world, and his alertness to changing business practices have enabled him to become a leader in the weaving industry. At the same time, his local roots and the Ortegas' eight-generation weaving heritage have remained of utmost importance to him. Now retired, he can survey what he has accomplished and become his sons' advisor as they carry on a thriving Ortega family business. (Pp. 248–53)

—Helen R. Lucero

CHAPTER ELEVEN

Summary

History provides no crystal ball that lets us see into the future. What we do know is that New Mexico is a product of its past. Its history is the story of its land and its people. Its history is the story of how its people, both old and new, have adjusted to the land. It is the story of how New Mexicans have adjusted to changing times and changing conditions.

In 1912 New Mexico became the 47th state. Its constitution, drawn up in 1910, outlined state government. It separated the powers of government among three branches. Only men could vote at first. After 1920 the women of New Mexico also became involved in politics.

Once it had become a state, New Mexico and its people got caught up in world events. The first of these involved United States relations with Mexico. In 1916 Pancho Villa's men raided Columbus, New Mexico. The United States responded by sending troops into Mexico. The next event was World War I. New Mexicans fought in the war. They also aided the war effort at home. New Mexico, like the rest of the world, also suffered from the Spanish flu epidemic.

In the 1920s many artists moved to New Mexico. Indeed, art colonies grew up in both Santa Fe and Taos. At each place both writers and painters gathered. Also creating artistic works were Indian and Hispanic New Mexicans.

In the 1920s Pueblo Indians also became involved in politics. The question of Pueblo land ownership led to the Bursum Bill. This bill caused the Pueblo Indians to unite. They opposed the Bursum Bill and succeeded in defeating it. In 1924 Congress passed the Pueblo Lands Act. This law protected Pueblo lands from outsiders. Also in that year, all Indians gained American citizenship.

During the Great Depression New Mexicans suffered like other Americans. Part of the state lay within the Dust Bowl. Farmers and ranchers were hard hit. So were the villagers of northern New Mexico. Many New Mexicans went to work for the New Deal relief programs. The hard times lasted through the 1930s.

In World War II New Mexicans were among the first to fight. This was true of the young men stationed in the Philippines. Many of them died on the Bataan Death March. The Navajo Code Talkers also helped the war effort. In 1945 the state became the birthplace of the atomic age. It became one of our country's major centers for weapons research.

Since the end of the war, New Mexico's economy has changed. Tourism became more important. Farming, ranching, and mining declined. Also since the war, New Mexico's people changed. The population has grown. People have moved into the state in great numbers. The changes in New Mexico since World War II have affected all New Mexicans. Yet after more than 400 years of recorded history, New Mexico is still a special land. It became a leading center for the arts. It is a land in which different cultures have thrived side by side. It is a land in which its oldest cultures continue to cherish their traditions and their heritages.

New Mexico's state motto is "We Grow as We Go" (*Crescit Eundo*). That means that New Mexicans have a positive outlook on the future. They expect the state to grow and move forward.

In 2012 the state will celebrate the one-hundred-year anniversary of statehood.

As we approach 2012, we should reflect on how New Mexicans have served their state and made it what it is today. In *Our New Mexico* you have been introduced to people and ideas important throughout the twentieth century.

These people, together with all New Mexicans, left us a legacy of accomplishment. They all were part of how New Mexico fulfilled its motto to "Grow as We Go." The choices made in the past one hundred years about the three themes discussed in this book—resources, culture, and continuity amid change—influence us to this day.

Many notable people contributed to making New Mexico's history since 1912. You have met many already in reading *Our New Mexico*. One more such person is going to be introduced: Senator Clinton P. Anderson. He served in the U.S. Senate from 1949 to 1972.

If you add fifty years to 1912, when New Mexico became a state, you have a date in the early 1960s. That is also the era Senator Anderson worked in Congress. He helped New Mexicans and all Americans have better lives. Looking at his career at the mid-point of the state's one-hundred-year anniversary is a way to understand how his service is a model for all of us. He was deeply concerned about the three themes of this book: resources, culture, and continuity amid change. He left a truly rich record in each of these areas, as you will see in the selection that follows. He was a great friend to the environment; he embraced peoples of all backgrounds; and he worked on social issues to continue what is good and improve what could be made better. He made a positive difference in his time, and his good work remains with us today.

We can all contribute in some manner. Few of us will ever become a U.S. Senator, but we are all citizens and can make a difference by what we do. We must be informed about the issues of our times, vote when we are eligible, help out in our communities, and be tolerant and accepting of others. These are the responsibilities of citizenship. They are also the way we help New Mexico "Grow as We Go."

SELECTION FROM
Conservation Politics
The Senate Career of Clinton P. Anderson

On the evening of May 20, 1963, the main ballroom of Washington D.C.'s Statler Hilton Hotel resounded to the animated conversation of a festive dinner party for the United States Senator from New Mexico Clinton P. Anderson. As the 650 guests settled back from their meal of braised beef and turned their attention to the head table, itself thronged with eighty dignitaries, representatives of twelve leading American conservation organizations stepped forward to bestow on the New Mexico Democrat the National Conservation Award. Among those present on that mild spring evening were one-third of the Senate's membership, three cabinet officers, dozens of House members, and scores of federal officials, lobbyists, and private citizens engaged in the advancement of the nation's natural resources conservation policies.

Earlier in the day, President John F. Kennedy, in a Rose Garden ceremony, saluted the sixty-seven-year-old senator for a lifetime of dedication to conservation. . . . Four days earlier, Senate and House negotiators had quickly compromised their differences over legislation to establish a major federal program to accelerate development of outdoor recreation facilities. They hoped to have the measure ready so that the president could sign it at the time of the tribute to Anderson, its principal architect. Numerous speakers at the evening banquet cited this act as well as dozens of Anderson's other conservation achievements. These ranged from development of New Mexico's vital water entitlements to a broad, nationally oriented program of wilderness preservation, water resources research, and land use planning. . . .

By any measure, New Mexico's Clinton Anderson (1895–1975) ranks as one of the most powerful and effective members of the United States Senate during the 1950s and early 1960s. . . . Clinton Anderson's imprint appears on a wide range of major post–World War II legislation, including measures promoting health care for the elderly, peaceful uses of atomic energy, and exploration of outer space. . . . But throughout his rich and productive career, Anderson's greatest satisfaction came from his success in forging new directions in America's natural resources policy. (Pp. x–12)

—Richard Allan Baker

Works Cited

Baker, Richard Allan. *Conservation Politics: The Senate Career of Clinton P. Anderson*. Albuquerque: University of New Mexico Press, 1985.

Barnett, Louise K. and James L. Thorson, eds. *Leslie Marmon Silko: A Collection of Critical Essays*. Albuquerque: University of New Mexico Press, 2001.

Cabeza de Baca, Fabiola. *We Fed Them Cactus*. Albuquerque: University of New Mexico Press, 1954.

Chávez, Thomas. *New Mexico's History: A Message for the Future*. Albuquerque: University of New Mexico Press, forthcoming.

deBuys, William. *Enchantment and Exploitation: The Life and Hard Times of a New Mexico Mountain Range*. Albuquerque: University of New Mexico Press, 1985.

Dillingham, Rick. *Fourteen Families in Pueblo Pottery*. Albuquerque: University of New Mexico Press, 1994.

Etulain, Richard, ed. *Contemporary New Mexico, 1940–1990*. Albuquerque: University of New Mexico Press, 1994.

Flynn, Kathryn A., ed. *New Mexico Blue Book*, 2003-2004. Santa Fe: Officeof the Secretary of State, 2003

Gómez-Quiñones, Juan. *Chicano Politics: Reality and Promise, 1940–1990*. Albuquerque: University of New Mexico Press, 1990.

Gonzales-Berry, Erlinda and David R. Maciel, eds. *The Contested Homeland: A Chicano History of New Mexico*. Albuquerque: University of New Mexico Press, 2000.

Greenberg, Henry and Georgia Greenberg. *Carl Gorman's World*. Albuquerque: University of New Mexico Press, 1984.

Griffin-Pierce, Trudy. *Native Peoples of the Southwest*. Albuquerque: University of New Mexico Press, 2000.

Hain, Paul L., F. Chris Garcia, and Gilbert K. St. Clair, eds. *New Mexico Government*, Third Edition. Albuquerque: University of New Mexico Press, 1994.

Hillerman, Tony and Ernie Bulow. *Talking Mysteries: A Conversation with Tony Hillerman*. Albuquerque: University of New Mexico Press, 2004.

Hoerig, Karl A. *Under the Palace Portal: Native American Artists in Santa Fe*. Albuquerque: University of New Mexico Press, 2003.

Hovey, Kathryn. *Anarchy and Community in the New American West: Madrid, New Mexico, 1970–2000*. Albuquerque: University of New Mexico Press, 2005.

Iverson, Peter. *Diné: A History of the Navajos*. Albuquerque: University of New Mexico Press, 2002.

Lamar, Howard. *The Far Southwest, 1846–1912: A Territorial History*. Revised Edition. Albuquerque: University of New Mexico Press, 2000.

Lomelí, Francisco A., Victor A. Sorell, and Genaro M. Padilla, eds. *Nuevomexicano Cultural Legacy: Forms, Agencies, and Discourse*. Albuquerque: University of New Mexico Press, 2002.

Lovato, Andrew Leo. *Santa Fe Hispanic Culture: Preserving Identity in a Tourist Town*. Albuquerque: University of New Mexico Press, 2004.

McCracken, Ellen, ed. *Fray Angélico Chávez: Poet, Priest, and Artist*. Albuquerque: University of New Mexico Press, 2000.

McCutcheon, Chuck. *Nuclear Reactions: The Politics of Opening a Radioactive Waste Disposal Site*. Albuquerque: University of New Mexico Press, 2002.

Montaño, Mary. *Tradiciones Nuevomexicanas: Hispano Arts and Culture of New Mexico* Albuquerque: University of New Mexico Press, 2001.

Myers, Joan. *Pie Town Woman*. Albuquerque: University of New Mexico Press, 2001.

Nieto-Phillips, John M. *The Language of Blood: The Making of Spanish-American Identity in New Mexico, 1880s–1930s*. Albuquerque: University of New Mexico Press, 2004.

Pike, David. *Roadside New Mexico: A Guide to Historic Markers*. Albuquerque: University of New Mexico Press, 2004.

Reed, Maureen. *A Woman's Place: Women Writing New Mexico*. Albuquerque: University of New Mexico Press, 2005.

Rivera, José A. *Acequia Culture*: *Water, Land, and Community in the Southwest*. Albuquerque: University of New Mexico Press, 1998.

Rudnick, Lois Palken, ed. *Intimate Memories: The Autobiography of Mabel Dodge Luhan*. Albuquerque: University of New Mexico Press, 1999.

Schneider-Hector, Dietmar. *White Sands: A History of a National Monument*. Albuquerque: University of New Mexico Press, 1993.

Simmons, Marc. *New Mexico: An Interpretive History*. Albuquerque: University of New Mexico Press, 1977.

Szasz, Ferenc M. *The Day the Sun Rose Twice: The Story of the Trinity Site Nuclear Explosion July 16, 1945*. Albuquerque: University of New Mexico Press, 1984.

Vanderwood, Paul J. and Frank N. Samponaro. *Border Fury: A Picture Postcard Record of Mexico's Revolution and U.S. War Preparedness, 1910–1917*. Albuquerque: University of New Mexico Press, 1988.

Weigle, Marta and Peter White. *The Lore of New Mexico*. Albuquerque: University of New Mexico Press, 2003.

Wilson, Norma C. *The Nature of Native American Poetry*. Albuquerque: University of New Mexico Press, 2001.

Wirth, John D. and Linda Harvey Aldrich. *Los Alamos—The Ranch School Years, 1917–1943*. Albuquerque: University of New Mexico Press, 2003.

Wyaco, Virgil. *A Zuni Life: A Pueblo Indian in Two Worlds*. Albuquerque: University of New Mexico Press, 1998.

Index